C000026838

The Shadow of the Gallows

Crime and Punishment on Tyneside
in the Eighteenth Century

Barry Redfern

Tyne Bridge Publishing
Newcastle Libraries & Information Service

Acknowledgments:

I am indebted to the following for access to books, records and other papers, and advice, support and encouragement – the staff of the Public Record Office, the Prison Service College Library at Wakefield, Teesside Archives, Tyne and Wear Archives, Northumberland Record Office, Newcastle Libraries, Mrs Beryl Sanderson of Warkworth, Desmond Walton of Newcastle, Mrs Mary McLoughlin, Northumbria Police Press Office, and the members of our local history societies and other organisations too numerous to name. But, first and last my thanks go to my wife Sheila for her deep support and tolerance of the disruption of family life that goes hand-in-hand with a project of this kind.

Barry Redfern, 2003

Illustrations acknowledgments: unless otherwise indicated illustrations are reproduced from the collections of Newcastle Libraries & Information Service.
The map on the inside covers is reproduced from Charles Hutton's map of Newcastle, 1769.

©Barry Redfern, 2003

Published by
City of Newcastle upon Tyne
Education & Libraries Directorate
Newcastle Libraries & Information Service
Tyne Bridge Publishing
2003

www.tynebridgepublishing.co.uk

ISBN 1-85795-176-X

All rights reserved. No part of this book may be reproduced, stored or introduced into a retrieval system or transmitted in any way or by any means (electronic, mechanical, photocopying, recording or otherwise) without the prior permission of the publishers.

Printed by Elanders Hindson, North Tyneside

Contents

Introduction

In the United Kingdom in the 18th century there were five basic ways of punishing offenders and preventing crime, starting with public humiliation, labour, pain and banishment. But it was the shadow of the gallows that lay across the century. Death was seen as the appropriate punishment for many offenders, and as a deterrent to others. There were more than 200 capital crimes on the statute book.

Life was harsh by today's standards and what emerges from this research into local archives is that many people were not deterred from crime by this strategy. Law enforcement was rudimentary and still rooted in the concept of the community in the parish dealing with their own crime problems. The investigations into the crimes described here were carried out without trained personnel, modern communications, transport, pathologists and scientists and the myriad benefits of such things as fingerprint evidence and DNA.

We know from academic research by Gwenda Morgan and Peter Rushton (see reading list) that crime in our region was neither better nor worse than elsewhere in the country. But there was public anxiety and fear of crime very clearly reported in the local newspapers of the period. Things did improve slowly in the 19th century, with changes in punishments, developing police forces, prisons and so forth, and the rise of a generally more humane view of how to treat our fellow man despite his misconduct.

Retirement from the local police force gave me the time to make use of the wealth of local and national records about life in the North East in the 18th century and to take a close look at how the criminal justice strategy worked in practice on Tyneside. What follows is much reduced from the mass of detail in the original research, however, the original script and other material will in time be made available to the public at Local Studies, Newcastle City Library, Newcastle upon Tyne.

There were some exciting discoveries to be made along the way such as the exact location of the Town Gallows and an old name for the Drunkard's Cloak. I had much pleasure from sharing everything with thousands of people in my talks from 1990 until I gave up in 2000. I will always be grateful to the staff of Newcastle Libraries and Information Service, and to Anna Flowers and Vanessa Histon of Tyne Bridge Publishing for making this information more widely available to the public.

And before you begin ... a hair-raising tale

In the course of giving many talks to the public one hears unexpected and sometimes strange stories. At the end of one of my talks a lady spoke to me and said she had been fascinated by the information about the exact location of the Town Moor Gallows for Newcastle upon Tyne and the connection to the site of the military barracks (see Gallows and Hangmen pages 32-34). She told me that after the second world war she had lived in married quarters in Fenham Barracks, Newcastle upon Tyne and what I said had explained something that had bothered her for years. She said "Every time I passed the place you have described inside the barracks where the gallows used to be, my hair would stand on end and I had the most uncomfortable feeling, There was no reason why that should be, but at last I understand it!"

Barry Redfern, Newcastle upon Tyne, 2003

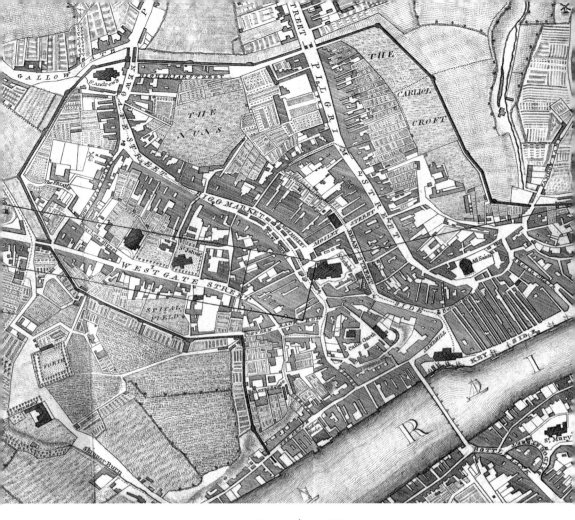

Newcastle in 1788.

1 Assize Week

ASSIZE WEEK
THE
HIGH SHERIFF
of the COUNTY of
NORTHUMBERLAND,

DESIRES the favour of his Friends and Acquaintances to meet him at the MOOT-HALL on Monday 17th Day of August inst. and from thence to accompany him to the usual Place of meeting the JUDGES of ASSIZE.

P.S. It has been found by Experience, that so many mistakes and omissions have happened in addressing and delivering LETTERS to INDIVIDUALS on this Occasion, that it is now thought proper to give no other Invitation than this general one.

Newcastle Journal Saturday 15 August 1767

Assize Week, was one of the key annual events in the 18th century social calendar of Newcastle upon Tyne and Northumberland, a time for a great gathering of North East families into the ancient walled town, for social events, business and trade, and for the annual visit of the Judges of Assize to clear the gaols of the town and county.

On the occasion in 1767, trumpeted above, the High Sheriff, landowner Hylton Lawson of Chirton near Tynemouth, issued the traditional invitation to the gentlemen of the county to gather at the Moot Hall in Castlegarth to follow the age old practice of meeting the judges at Gateshead and escorting them to the courts at Newcastle and to their lodgings.

Newcastle in 1745, from a drawing by Buck. The Keep is to the left of St Nicholas' church (it became a cathedral in 1882) with the old Moot Hall in Castlegarth just to the right of the Keep.

The judges visited Newcastle at Lamas at the beginning of August. In the 18th century, the Judges of the High Courts of England travelled the country in what are still called circuits – groups of the courts in the principal county towns. The Kings Justices presided over Assize Courts, the senior level of court in the provinces, to hear civil causes, to hear and determine serious crime cases and to clear the gaols of prisoners and ensure that no one was held imprisoned without trial.

The circuit for the North East usually began at York with separate courts for the city and the county; then continued north for the Durham Assizes, and on to Newcastle. The judges then travelled on to Carlisle to clear the gaols of Cumberland and Westmoreland, ending with the Assizes at Lancaster before they returned south to London.

Escorting the judges was not just a matter of protocol or courtesy. The escorts protected the Kings Justices from the real dangers of travel in England and Wales at that time.

In 1400, King Henry IV made Newcastle upon Tyne a town and county in its own right, separating it from Northumberland for local government purposes. The new town and county acquired many rights including the right to a sheriff, a separate sitting of the Court of Assize, and for Newcastle to have its own gaol and put up a gallows to hang criminals. In fact there had been gaols at Newcastle and a gallows on the Town Moor for many years before 1400.

THE POOR BURGESSES' CATECHISM

Who are you?

– A poor burgess of Newcastle.

What is Newcastle?

– A county of itself and corporation by charter; governed by a Mayor, ten aldermen, Recorder, Sheriff, Town Clerk, Sword and Mace Bearer, 6 sergeants at Mace etc.

What do you get by its being a county of itself?

– The honour of feeding the judges at the Assizes and keeping the gallows in repair.

What do get by your sheriff?

– The honour of being attended up Gallowgate by a brother burgess.

From An Essay on Charters of Newcastle upon Tyne *by John Collier 1777.*

The Keep at Newcastle, and the Castlegarth area, remained part of the county of Northumberland – a small island of county land in the middle of the town. The Courts of Assize for Northumberland, and some sittings of the county Quarter Sessions Court, were held at the Moot Hall in Castlegarth, requiring careful observance of boundaries and areas of responsibility. After 1400 Castlegarth became a haven for criminals wanted in Newcastle. Justices and other officials of Newcastle had no right to arrest wanted persons in that tiny piece of land so densely packed with houses and other buildings. This state of affairs continued until 1589 when it was stopped by charter of Elizabeth I.

Usually the Kings Justices travelled to Newcastle from Durham on a Saturday, the exact time of arrival at the Gateshead boundary being arranged by the under-sheriff for Northumberland. He also provided the judges with lists of the prisoners and the charges against them. During the Saturday morning many of the gentlemen would attend a service in St Nicholas' church to raise funds for Newcastle Infirmary, followed by lunch at one of the famous inns in Newgate Street.

After lunch the High Sheriff would go to the Moot Hall to greet the gentlemen who were joining him to set out to meet the judges formally. It must have been quite a sight to watch as many as 300 men with horses and up to 30 or 40 carriages passing through Black Gate into Castlegarth. The numbers of carriages are confirmed in the diary of a fifteen year-old apprentice hostman (a controller of river trade) in 1750: 'Monday the 13th (i.e. of August 1750) Got up early in the Morning and went to Winkhamlee, came home got upon the Chappell Leads and saw the High Sheriff go out, there was twenty-nine Coaches and Chariots went out to meet My Lord Judge.' (The Journals of Ralph Jackson 1749-1756)

The judges' carriage around 1910.

The High Sheriff of Northumberland provided wine, pipes and tobacco inside the Moot Hall and the gentlemen would take a glass of wine, smoke a pipe then move out to make space for the others until the time arrived for the procession to form up.

Saturday last the stewards of the Infirmary were met at the Exchange by Edward Collingwood Esq., High Sheriff for the County of Northumberland, and several Gentlemen, from whence they proceeded to St Nicholas Church, where a sermon for the Benefit of that charity was preached by the Rev. Mr. Wilson Vicar of Corbridge, from Proverbs. Chap. xix, v. 17, after which a very genteel company dined with them at Brodies Long Room. The collection at the church amounted to £22 3s 6d.

Newcastle Courant, Saturday, 11th August 1787

First came the Bailiffs with their Rods in pairs, then two trumpeters decorated with banners and ribbands, then the Gaoler with his Black Rod, the Under Sheriff with his white Rod and Sword, the High Sheriff with his Rod and Sword and two pages to hold his stirrups, then gentlemen and servants. All formed up behind the High Sheriff's coach and six, followed by the Mayor's coach and all other coaches and carriages. The procession moved off through Black Gate, then down Side to cross the Tyne Bridge.

Sheriff Hill in Gateshead is so-called because for centuries the

Mansion House, Newcastle

Thomas Miles Richardson's painting of the Sheriff's procession on the Side in 1835.

procession passed up the steep bank towards the Gateshead boundary to meet the Kings Justices. They continued their journey until they reached the the Cannon inn and waited there to greet the judges arriving from Durham. Formalities included a requirement that the judges sit facing forward and the High Sheriff sit with his back to the horses during the journey down to Newcastle.

The High Sheriff's procession always halted at the Blue Stone on the Tyne

The Guildhall Court in 1952, the first sitting of the Court of Assize since 1882.

Bridge which marked the boundary between Newcastle on the north bank and the land belonging to the County Palatine of Durham to the South. Here the judges were greeted by the Town Sheriff of Newcastle supported by other officials and gentlemen of the town. The procession then moved on to the Guildhall in Sandhill.

Late in 1771, extreme weather forced a break with tradition when the Tyne Bridge was swept away in the tumultuous floods of that winter. Ferries were set up to meet the needs of trade and travel and the following year in Assize Week new arrangements were made for greeting the judges. In 1773 a temporary bridge across the Tyne was completed and the *Newcastle Courant* reported that the judges had been met at the usual place.

Usually the judges were met by the Mayor and Aldermen of Newcastle at the foot of the stairs leading to the Guildhall Court, then, with full ceremony and regalia, they made their way into the court room. The Guildhall Court still exists and is a fine example of an early court. The Guildhall itself was erected between 1655 and 1658 by a York architect, Robert Trollop, acquiring a new facade in the 19th century. The judges formally opened the Assize, then adjourned that sitting of the Assizes until after the weekend, and proceeded to the Moot Hall in Castlegarth where they repeated the ceremony.

The Northumberland Assize Court was built in the 13th century, and by the mid 18th century was long past its best. Formerly known as the Great Hall of the King, or the Shire Hall, it was by then known as the Moot Hall and stood just north of the site of the present Moot Hall. It was used each year for the Northumberland Assizes and

The 13th century Moot Hall on Castlegarth. Below, a plan of the Castlegarth in 1746.

> The Gentlemen made a grand procession with the High Sheriff to the moot hall, where it was agreed on the want of a bridge that the High Sheriff should walk accompanied by his company and followed by his coach and six, with a grand retinue to the Sandhill to receive the Judges of Assize. Christopher Wilkinson Esq. Sheriff of this Town in the Mayor's Barge attended by several Gentlemen in the River Jury Barge went and received the Judges on the South Shore and landed them on the Key opposite the Exchange, which they walked through and were received at the foot of the Court Stairs by the Right Worshipful Sir Walter Blackett Bart., Mayor and Magistrates.
>
> *Newcastle Courant* Saturday 22nd August 1772

occasionally for sittings of the Northumberland Quarter Sessions. At the south end was another smaller building known as the Grand Jury Room used by the Grand Jury, a group of twenty-four prominent gentlemen, chaired by a foreman who was usually one of the baronets of the county. Their task was to review the evidence supporting the bills of indictment at the Assizes and decide if they should go forward for a full trial before the judge and jury. If the Grand Jury decided there was a sound case the indictment document would be declared 'billa vera' (true bill). If not, then 'ignoramus' was announced and the prisoners would be discharged without trial.

From time to time the Moot Hall was used as a theatre with permission from the Northumberland justices.

By the year 1787 complaints about the state of the Moot Hall had reached the stage of formal representations at the Assizes, but it was 1810 before it was closed and demolished. The County Assizes for the summer of 1810 and 1811 were held in St Nicholas' church. In August 1812 the first Northumberland Assizes were held in the new Moot Hall and High Court trials have continued there until the present day.

After the ceremony in the Moot Hall the judges were escorted to the Mansion House where they were accommodated during their six or seven day stay at Newcastle. The Mansion House was the official residence of the Mayor and stood on the Quayside on a piece of land next to the site of the present day Copthorne Hotel. Dating from 1691, the building provided a high standard of comfort, hospitality and entertainment for the judges during their stay. It was sold by the corporation in 1837 and was used for other purposes until it was destroyed by fire in 1895.

On the Sunday of Assize Week, 'Assize Sunday' as it was known, the judges, in

The Mansion House, c.1836. It was sold in 1837 and burned down in 1895.

their splendid robes, were escorted in a grand procession from the Mansion House to attend the service at St Nicholas' while huge crowds turned out to watch.

Prisoners for trial at the Northumberland Assizes were brought from the County Gaol at Morpeth to the Keep at Newcastle. The Rev. John Baillie writing in 1801 felt that the treatment of these untried prisoners was an 'outrage on justice':

> A man is to be accounted 'guilty' till he is legally proven to be 'innocent', which is frequently the case. His punishment, viz. being manacled, conveyed through the public streets fixed on a cart, thrown into this den of filth, covered only with a little straw, chained to the wall, and shewn like a wild beast, to the gaping mob, by a rapacious gaoler at two-pence a-piece; his punishment, supposing him acquitted, is then only to cease. To the credit, however, of the present county gaoler, Mr. Blake, it is at least justice to remark that the unfeeling and sordid practice of exposing the unhappy prisoners to public view has been for some years discontinued.

> *An Impartial History of Newcastle upon Tyne*, John Baillie, 1801

The guardroom of the Keep in the late 19th century. It had been renovated by then, but the bleak conditions can be imagined.

John Howard, the 18th century prison reformer, gave a moving description of the conditions for prisoners in the dungeon of the Keep at Castlegarth:

> Gaol delivery once a year. Assize held at Newcastle, wither prisoners are conveyed; and men and women confined together seven or eight nights in a dirty damp dungeon down six steps in the old castle, which having no roof, in a wet season the water is some inches deep. The felons are chained to rings in the wall.

The State of the Prisons, John Howard, 1792

On Assize Sunday the public could pay the gaoler sixpence to view the prisoners chained to walls in the dungeon of the 'old castle'.

These images provide a stark contrast to the intense social activity of Assize

Week. After the splendid service at the church of St Nicholas the judges and many others were entertained by one of the senior gentlemen of the area:

> About one o'clock on Sunday last Mr. Baron Clarke and Mr. Baron Smythe accompanied by a great many gentlemen went to Fenham, where an elegant dinner was provided for them by William Orde Esq.
>
> Sunday afternoon, Sir Matthew White Ridley Bart., gave an elegant Fete Champetre, in his grounds at Heaton. The Judges and a splendid number of Ladies and Gentlemen were present. Four marquees were pitched on the occasion and a select Band of Music provided.
>
> *Newcastle Courant* 25th August 1750

> On Tuesday Sir M.W. Ridley, Bart., gave a splendid Fete Champetre at his seat at Heaton, near this town. His Royal Highness Prince William of Gloucester was amongst the guests, who were very numerous and consisted of nearly all the fashion which the Music Festival and the Assizes had brought to town.
>
> *Newcastle Courant* 30th July 1796

In 1787 another distinguished visitor, the Duke of Northumberland, was at Newcastle for Assize Week and in common with other senior figures of the county made gifts of money to the gaols for the benefit of poor prisoners.

A further Assize Week tradition was for the Mayor of Newcastle to take the judges from Newcastle to Tynemouth and back in the Mayor's Barge, an ornate craft rowed by oarsmen with a Northumbrian piper in the bows. It sounds an idyllic trip but there was an occasion in the 18th century when sharp words between the

The Mayor's Barge in 1903 just before it was hoisted out of the water for the last time.

Mayor and one of the judges, Mr. Justice Page, led to cancellation of these trips for several years.

On another occasion, one of the judges slipped into the water as he stepped from the barge inspiring *My Lord Size*, a popular comical song of around 1806. The judge in the song is carried 'to the dead house' on the Quayside, assumed to be drowned but stages a miraculous recovery and 'then the coach and the trumpeters came with great speed, and back to the Mansion House carried Lord Size.' Sir Robert Graham, Bart., is thought to be the judge who actually fell into the Tyne, but the newspapers of the day carried no reports of it.

Two of the key events of Assize Week were dinners given in honour of the judges by the Mayor of Newcastle upon Tyne and the High Sheriff of Northumberland. The 'Assembly Room' was opened in the Groat Market in 1736.

> THURSDAY the High Sheriff gave a sumptuous and elegant Entertainment at the Assembly-room to a numerous Company of Noblemen and Gentlemen, amongst whom were the Right Hon. the Earls of Northumberland and Darlington, the Lords Ravensworth and Barnard &c. There was the grandest Desert ever served up on the Occasion, in which there were four dozen of Pine-Apples.
>
> *Newcastle Courant* Saturday 2nd August 1755

Assembly rooms and the long rooms in various inns at Newcastle were the venues for the other kinds of entertainment and diversion offered during this festive week. Parker's Long Room, for example was in the Turks Head Inn (proprietor William Parker) at the upper end of the Bigg Market and was said to be the largest public room in Newcastle when it was

The new Assembly Rooms opened in 1776 on Westgate Road.

built onto the inn in 1747. Space was often limited, however, so members of society were invited to subscribe towards the building of the new Assembly Rooms which opened on 24th June 1776 and contained a ball room, supper room, card rooms and other rooms for private use. It still stands today on Westgate Road.

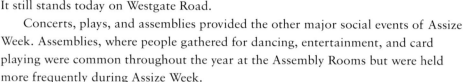

Concerts, plays, and assemblies provided the other major social events of Assize Week. Assemblies, where people gathered for dancing, entertainment, and card playing were common throughout the year at the Assembly Rooms but were held more frequently during Assize Week.

THERE WILL BE ASSEMBLIES ON THE
Tuesday, Wednesday and Thursday in the Assize Week,
AND ON THE Tuesday Fortnights afterwards as usual.
NEWCASTLE,
August 19th, 1767,
THERE WILL BE A CONCERT OF MUSIC
At Mr. Parker's Long Room,
On Wednesday morning the 19th inst., and will begin at Half an Hour after Eleven. TICKETS (at 3s. each) may be had at Mr. Parker's, Mr. Hawthorn's, Mr. Barber's and at Mr. Avison's in Green Court, Newgate Street.

Newcastle Journal *Saturday 15th August 1767. Mr. Avison was Charles Avison, (1709-1776) the famous Newcastle musician, composer, teacher and organist at St Nicholas'.*

A rising young barrister, Nicholas Ridley, age 25, younger brother of the first baronet Sir Matthew White Ridley of Blagdon, kept a diary in Assize Week 1773:

Monday 9th August 1773

Dined with Mr. Mayor, drank tea at Mrs. Widdrington's.
Went to town with Gov'r &c., attended the Court, went to dinner at half past 2, came away before 6, dressed and went to the Assembly, danced with B. Allgood, slept in Westgate.

Tuesday 10th August 1773

Dined with the Recorder, supped at Wind's.
Went to court at 7 o'clock, left it at 1, dressed and went to dinner. To the con-

cert at 7, from thence with Bolton and Story to supper, met with an adventure, got home at 12.

Wednesday 11th August 1773
Dined with the High Sheriff, drank tea at Mrs. Widdrington's.
In court in the morning, went to the town moor at 10, played a good match at Cricket, returned to dinner at 3, dressed and went to the Assembly, went down one dance with Mrs. Moncaster.

Thursday 12th August 1773
Dined with Mr. Justice Chambers, supped with my partner.
In court in the morning, dined at 3 o'clock, afterwards called at Sir W. Blackett's, called on Mrs. Ward, dressed for the Assembly, danced with Miss H. Allgood.

Friday 13th August 1773
Dined at Brampton, supped at Carlisle.
Set out with Norton and Lowes in a Postchaise at 7 o'clock, met our brethren at Chollerford, took horse and rode to Brampton by 3, arrived safe at Carlisle about 9.

The next few days were spent in similar fashion at the Carlisle Assizes but included the highlight of a first brief for the young barrister. The cryptic note for Tuesday night 'met with an adventure' is surely a mysterious coded entry for the reader to unravel!

Amidst this flurry of social activity, the real function of Assize Week went on, and the judges worked at the Guildhall and Moot Hall Courts clearing the gaols of town and county of prisoners and dealing with civil actions. The number of prisoners awaiting trial varied widely across the 18th century and not all of them were convicted. For example, in 1740 29 prisoners awaited trial at Newcastle, while in 1765 there were five, and in 1793 only one. In contrast, at Northumberland Assizes in 1740, four awaited trial, in 1765 there were nine, and in 1793 there were 11.

All cases committed to the Assize Courts were essentially serious matters in the sense that the majority carried the death penalty for at the end of the 18th century more than 200 crimes were capital offences. However, the judges would often pronounce the death sentence but reprieve some prisoners before they left the town. *Newcastle Journal* for Saturday 1 August 1752 notes 'Thomas Gowery, for stealing a Horse, and sentenced to be hanged at the last Assizes, but reprieved, transported for fourteen years.'

The range of crimes charged against a sample 194 prisoners between 1736 and

1793 included assault, burglary, forgery, highway robbery, house-breaking, murder, manslaughter obtaining goods by deceit, rape, attempted rape, riot, selling corn short of measure, shop-breaking, stealing (horses, cattle, sheep and game), and wounding.

The sentences handed out for these crimes included nine hanged, 25 sentenced to death but reprieved for transportation, six whipped, 12 branded, one fined, three fined and sent to the House of Correction, and 59 were acquitted.

The numbers of persons actually executed for criminal offences in Northumberland, Newcastle and Berwick upon Tweed during the 18th century amounted to 18 men and one woman hanged at Morpeth, ten men and two women hanged at Westgate (both Northumberland), 13 men and two women hanged on Newcastle Town Moor, one man hung at Newgate, and one man and one woman hanged at Berwick upon Tweed.

Murder and horse-stealing were the crimes for which most of these 49 men were hanged, though highway robbery, burglary, house-breaking, arson, riot, rape, coining, shop-breaking, sheep stealing, and returning unlawfully from transportation were also hanging offences. The six women were hanged for murder, house-breaking and burglary.

At the conclusion of the Assize Courts in 1793 the number of prisoners was the subject of comment in the press:

Our Assizes this week afforded small pickings for gentlemen of the long robe. The whole business, both in the civil and criminal matters, was finished at the Guildhall, before the Right Honourable Sir Archibald Macdonald, Lord Chief Baron of the Exchequer, on Monday, when Hannah Leighton, the only prisoner, charged on Coroner's Inquest, with the wilful murder of a male infant child, was acquitted. The business for the County of Northumberland, both on the Crown and Nisi Prius side, was all finished on Wednesday afternoon, and the Judges set off yesterday morning for Carlisle.

Newcastle Courant Saturday 3rd August 1793

It was the custom in the Tyneside newspapers of the 18th century simply to report the results of cases in the Assize Courts, with little background report or comment. There seemed to be an assumption that their readers would know the story of a criminal case from earlier reports of the crime concerned. But there were odd notes and short reports here and there which provide revealing (and sometimes tragic) images of court life:

> **Tuesday night (July 26th) during the trial respecting the Tone estate (a legacy dispute) two boys who had climbed into the Window of the Moot-hall fell a-sleep and loosing their hold, dropped to the ground, whereby one of them was killed, and the other had his leg broken and was otherwise much bruised.**
>
> *Newcastle Chronicle* Saturday 30th July 1785

Six years later came another almost farcical accident, this time at the Newcastle upon Tyne Assizes at the Guildhall:

> **On Tuesday (August 23rd) during the trial of T. Dunbar* at the Guildhall a general alarm was spread by the falling of a portion of the ceiling upon the green table; on which a scene of much confusion ensued by the crowd violently rushing out of the Hall, but fortunately none of them were much hurt, and when the tumult had subsided, a harmless laugh generally prevailed at the temporary losses of hats, wigs, caps, shoes, cloaks, shawls etc. This was occasioned by the curiosity of a person who had got upon the leads, from thence between the roof and the ceiling, and having missed his step, both his legs came through the ceiling and were seen by the people below. The present situation of the Guildhall from the recent dreadful accident**, contributed considerably to heighten the alarm. An eminent Council (sic) having secured himself under the table on being laughed at by his acquaintance very aptly replied 'My retreat proceeded only from the quickness of my apprehension!'**
>
> *Newcastle Courant* Saturday 27th August 1791
>
> (*charged with a Shipping Act offence on the Tyne and acquitted.
> **There had been a fire next door at St Thomas Chapel which had damaged the roof of the Guildhall.)

The 'green table' was a large oval table covered with green baize in the well of this old court room in front of the judge's seat, and remains there to this day.

Pickpockets were active in the Assize Courts at the Guildhall and the Moot Hall:

> **Monday (i.e. August 14th) a gentleman had his pocket picked at the Moothall, of his purse, containing near £30 in gold and silver, and two mourning rings. The same day, another gentleman, lost by the same means, as it is supposed, a draft of the value of £89.**
>
> *Newcastle Courant* Saturday 19th August 1786

However, given the opportunity, the judges made swift work of dealing with any pickpockets detected in their courts. On Tuesday 3rd August 1790, at the Moot Hall, Thomas Watson was on trial for the murder by shooting of man called George Gibson at Newham in Northumberland. The *Newcastle Courant* reported that another drama was being played out in the court during Watson's trial:

> **During the trial of Watson on Tuesday last at the Moot Hall, Jane Stephenson, an old offender, was detected picking pockets, and, on examination, several handkerchiefs were found concealed in her breast. She was immediately taken into custody, and as soon as the trial of Watson ended, was arraigned, convicted of the fact, and sentenced to seven years transportation.**
>
> **Several light fingered gentry seemed to have attended the northern circuit, some of them practiced with success at Durham and York, and Sunday a valuable watch was purloined from an unfortunate juror who had joined the crowd to view the procession to St Nicholas Church.**
>
> *Newcastle Courant* Saturday 7th August 1790

Given the recent history of pickpockets in North East courts there can be little doubt that the judge, Baron Thompson, would have been well satisfied to see this formal court record of his work that day:

Northumberland Assizes, Tuesday morning 3rd August 1790
before Baron Thompson – Thomas Watson (puts guilty*) for the wilful murder of George Gibson by shooting with a pistol at the parish of Bamburgh

23rd February last, also charged by the Coroner's Inquisition.

Jane Stephenson wife of Robert Stevenson (sic) for feloniously stealing one chequed linen handkerchief value 6d the property of John Gibson at the Castle of Newcastle upon Tyne 3rd August 1790 – in court – (puts Guilty*) Transported beyond the seas for seven years.

Northern Circuit Minute Book 1783-1790

(* 'puts guilty' is the 18th century court method of recording that the jury found the prisoner guilty of the charge.)

As Assize Week drew to a close and the judges prepared to depart for Carlisle there were one or possibly two presentations to be made to the judges. The first concerns what was known as a 'Maiden Assize'. Today the expression 'Maiden' applied to a court sitting would mean that there were no cases to be heard and it used to be the practice on such occasions to give a pair of white gloves to the presiding judge. In the 18th century a 'Maiden Assize' was one where no death sentences were passed by the judge. At the Newcastle Assizes the gloves were presented to more officials than the judge alone.

> **… This being a Maiden Assize for this Town, that is no criminals having sentence of death passed on them, the Judges and attendants were presented with white gloves by the corporation according to an established custom.**
>
> *Newcastle Chronicle or Weekly Advertiser*, Saturday 11th August 1787

The other presentation to the judges took place each year without exception. It was customary to present each Judge of Assize with an old gold coin before they departed for Carlisle. The gifts appear to have been simply a gesture of thanks and goodwill to the judges – after all, any fees would have been paid to the judges in current coin of the realm and not old gold coins. There are no records to support the notion that the coins were what has been popularly known as 'Dagger Money' or gold paid to the judges to buy, or in place of, weapons. During the 17th century it was customary for the High Sheriff of Northumberland to give a dagger and other gifts to the judges on departure from Newcastle upon Tyne.

Finally, it would not be fitting to end a description of Assize Week on Tyneside without piecing together the story of the murder of Ferdinando Forster and the hanging of John Fenwick in 1701. The original court records for that year have not survived but we can examine other sources such as this entry in church records at Newcastle:

22nd August 1701

fenwick Mr. John of Rock Stabd ffardinandoe foster Esq. Parlyment Man for Northumberld The Twenty second Aug Betwixt The Whitt Cros & The Thorntre

Burial Register of St Andrew's Church, Newcastle upon Tyne 1687 – 1705

or in modern English:

22nd August 1701, John Fenwick of Rock stabbed Ferdinando Forster, a Member of Parliament for Northumberland, the twenty-second of August between the White Cross and the Thorn tree.

The White Cross was a market cross in Newgate Street at the top of Low Friar Street. A thorn tree grew nearby. For a cleric to make such a note in the church registers was unusual and shows how shocked the people of the town were by this great scandal and tragedy.

According to historian John Brand the Assizes had already begun but which judge presided over the ensuing trial of Fenwick is not known. Given the serious nature of the crime about to unfold it would probably have been the senior judge, Lord Chief Baron Edward Ward, who took on that responsibility.

Ferdinando Forster was a member of the famous Northumberland county family the Forsters of Bamburgh. Aged 31, and unmarried, he was a Member of Parliament for Northumberland. John Fenwick, of Rock in Northumberland, was another prominent gentleman of the county and about the same age as Forster. He was a member of the Fenwick family who owned the village of Kenton, north of Newcastle, and its coal mines. John Fenwick

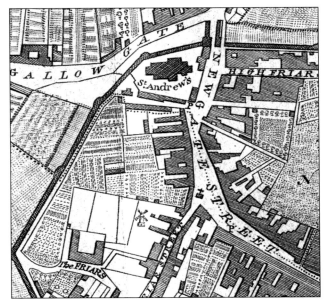

Gallowgate and the White Cross, marked by a small cross where Low Friar Street meets Newgate Street.

was reported to be a married man and his wife was pregnant at the time of his trial and execution.

Forster and Fenwick were in Newcastle for the Assize Week when a bitter dispute arose between the two men, probably over some family matter. Two versions of this tragic event have come down to us. All the essential details are the same except the day on which it happened. The first account appears in John Brand's *History of Newcastle upon Tyne* and that version is followed by Eneas Mackenzie in his *History of Newcastle upon Tyne*.

On the evening of Friday 22 August 1701 Ferdinando Forster was dining in the long room of the Black Horse inn on the west side of Newgate Street when he was 'called out' or challenged to a duel by John Hall of Otterburn on behalf of Fenwick. Forster accepted and went into Newgate Street where Fenwick was waiting between the White Cross and the thorn tree. Swords were drawn, but before the fight began Forster slipped and while he lay defenceless on the ground Fenwick stabbed Forster to death with his sword. Brand states that Fenwick stabbed Forster from behind as they were leaving the Black Horse Inn.

The Hall family of Otterburn lived in Otterburn Tower and it is quite probable that 'John Hall of Otterburn' mentioned above was John 'Mad Jack' Hall of Otterburn, a justice of the peace, who was arrested in Preston, Lancashire, in 1715 for High Treason after taking part in the Jacobite Rebellion of that year. John Hall was 44 when he was hanged at Tyburn in London on 13th July 1716.

The other version of the murder is attributed to Alderman Hugh Hornby and is quoted by John Sykes in his *Local Records, 1833*. The greater part of the Northumberland Grand Jury is said to have been with Forster in the long room of the Black Horse that evening when John Fenwick entered, singing a famous border song 'Sir John Fenwick's the Fairest Among Them'. The text of this song has been lost but the tune remains a favourite amongst Northumbrian pipers to the present day. The song provoked a quarrel between Fenwick and Forster, but with the help of friends the matter was smoothed over that night. However, the next day the two met near the White Cross, the quarrel flared up again, and Forster was killed by Fenwick.

Alderman Hornby says that John Fenwick was arrested in a garden at the back of Gallowgate or Sidgate (the ancient name for Percy Street). He was charged with murdering Ferdinando Forster and tried at the Newcastle Assizes sitting in the Guildhall Court overlooking the River Tyne. He was convicted and was sentenced to death by hanging.

Executions were held in public and the hanging of John Fenwick would, in the normal course of events, have taken place at the gallows on the Town Moor. There

Newgate Street in 1813, leading up to the gate and the prison.

was, however, a security problem. William Boutflower was the Town Sheriff and it was his legal responsibility to make sure the death sentence was carried out. Boutflower had information that coal miners at Kenton, loyal to John Fenwick, were planning stop the public execution from taking place. Newcastle was still a walled town and the gates and walls were intact and in good order so on Thursday 25th September 1701 Boutflower ordered the town to be sealed off by closing all the gates. They hanged John Fenwick in public in Newgate Street either from the thorn tree at the White Cross, or from a piece of timber put up between Newgate Gaol and the gaoler's house. The public hangman for Newcastle upon Tyne in 1701 was Thomas Cooper.

The cleric at St Andrew's Church recorded the event:

25 September 1701 ffenwick Mr. John of Rock Was hanged The 25 day of September 1701 for stabing Mr. ffardinando foster of Bambro A parlement Man.

Burial Register of St Andrew's Church, Newcastle upon Tyne 1687 – 1705

The murder of Ferdinando Forster was a double blow for his family because despite having three brothers, he was, by 1701, the sole surviving male heir of the Forsters of Bamburgh. Forster was buried at Bamburgh Parish Church and his armour – gloves, breastplate and helmet – hangs on metal brackets high up on the wall inside the church to the left of the altar. Nearby is a Forster family memorial

Duels to settle matters of honour were common enough although illegal. A death in a duel left the survivor and seconds liable to be charged with murder under British Common Law.

The judge and jury must have believed that Fenwick acted with dishonour and could neither excuse him nor extend clemency towards him. But something made the judge hesitate. An execution for murder at that time would be carried out promptly after trial, usually within a couple of days and there is no apparent explanation why the execution of Fenwick was held over until 25th September 1701.

All the attention of the time and the written accounts since then focus on Forster and Fenwick but the burial register of St Andrew's Church tells us that Fenwick was not the only man hanged at Newcastle upon Tyne that day for a similar offence – Thomas Leggerton a 'Whellwright was Hanged The 25 day of September 1701 for stabing a young man.' Leggerton was buried in the graveyard at St Andrew's Church.

An execution at Newgate, c.1817.

2 Gallows and Hangmen

THE COMMON COUNCIL BOOKS
OF NEWCASTLE UPON TYNE 1699-1718

At a Common Council held 25th December 1705.

Alexander Robinson. It is ordered that he be settled in the room of Thomas Cooper
and be the common executioner
in the hanging of felons, putting persons in the pillory,
in scourging the poor, clearing the streets of swine and
perform all other matters belonging to the place and duty of the hangman.

The town hangman at Newcastle from the 17th to 19th centuries was known as the Whipper and Hougher. Most of what is known about these hangmen comes from the Newcastle Chamberlain's Account Books. The first mention of the Whipper and Hougher occurs in May 1670 when the 'Whipper and Hougher of Swine' was paid 22 shillings for ten weeks' work, followed in August by the payment of £1 1s 8d for a quarter year salary.

'Hougher of Swine' meant a person who cut the sinews in the legs of swine to stop the animals wandering and causing a nuisance to residents. It is hard to imagine the chaotic state of town streets during those far off days. In 1596 Newcastle was afflicted with the plague and the town bellman was sent to warn people to keep 'doggs and swine' under control for fear of spreading infection. Then payments begin to appear in the account books to meet the costs of killing off wandering livestock.

During the space of a year or so the authorities killed not less than 126 dogs, plus many cats, pigs and poultry, all found wandering on the streets. The remains were buried outside the town walls.

The authorities also used the Whipper and Hougher to deal with beggars, rogues and vagabonds, usually by whipping or disfigurement through branding. It appears that the authorities were prepared to use the hangman's services for other community problems too:

> By the vigilance of the Magistrates of this town, upwards of thirty measures have lately been seized, and taken from some of those conscientious Hucksters who prey upon the vitals of the labouring poor; they, being all short of the legal standard, were on Friday se'nnight* burnt on the Sandhill by the hands of the common Hangman. One of those measures had a false bottom, which the upright owner could put up and down at pleasure. If any of those delinquents be again convicted of such infamous practices, it is hoped our worthy Magistrates will order their names to be published.
>
> *Newcastle Courant*, Saturday 10th October 1789
>
> * 'se'nnight', a week ago from Friday last i.e. Friday 2nd October 1789

Using the 'common hangman' to destroy the false measures was intended, presumably, to focus additional public humiliation on the fraudulent tradesmen.

After the Municipal Corporations Act of 1835, the Newcastle authorities adopted a different approach. Public hangmen were hired and brought in from elsewhere, notably Glasgow and York. Public transport had improved, making it much easier for an experienced executioner to travel. The practice was shared by other authorities creating a few provincial and semi-professional executioners.

Establishment of a national prison service in 1877 and other 19th century changes, such as discontinuing public executions and the introduction of the 'drop' apparatus – a gallows with a trap door, led to the Home Office taking control of executioners. Suitable applicants were given training to try to ensure that humane standards were observed.

What manner of man was attracted to the post of Whipper and Hougher? Little is known about them. But a 19th century report in the press about a public whipper sometimes casually employed by the authorities gives some hints:

NEWCASTLE POLICE. On Wednesday last (February 13th) Richard Coates, Robert Turnbull and Robert Cooper had the punishment of public whipping inflicted upon them, in the Manors, they having through the vigilance of one of the officers been apprehended as sturdy beggars and duly convicted. It came out in evidence before the sitting Magistrate that these men and two others not taken have for some time past infested the suburbs and unfrequented parts of the town and by intimidation extorted money from the female inhabitants under colour of being out of work and that after raising money in that unlawful way they have uniformly spent it in Alehouses. Coates and Turnbull were once keelmen but of late years have ceased to be so though sufficiently able to work. Cooper also an able bodied man has been employed as a Quayside labourer and occasionally as the 'public whipper'.

Newcastle Courant Saturday 16th February 1822

A classic example of the 'biter bit', or in this case the 'whipper whipped.'

Tradition has it that a British hangman's fee was the value of one Scottish mark – 13 and a half pence – and that 12 pence was for the hangman and a penny half-penny to buy the rope. In 165 years the salary of the Whipper and Hougher never varied from £1 1s 8d per quarter, which amounted to tenpence a week, although here and there extra fees were paid for whipping offenders and other tasks.

There had been a gallows on the Town Moor at Newcastle for centuries, probably since the first growth of a township. In 1357 the Gallows was used as one of the reference points to describe the boundaries of the Town Moor for an inquisition returned to Chancery (*History of Newcastle* by John Brand, 1789). This suggests the authorities regarded the gallows as a permanent, long established and fixed landmark in the town. The gallows was also used as a point of reference in 1620 for an inquisition by the Bishop of Durham into the condition of the castle.

Where exactly was the Town Gallows? Henry Bourne gives some details:

> The Suburbs out of Newgate Gray informs us, were ruined in the late Civil Wars. However the street Gallowgate (so called because of the Way that the Malefactors of the Town of Newcastle go to the Gallows, which is situated in a very low Place called the Gallows-hole) Is become again a very tollerable Street, and a very pleasant Place, having in it some good houses, which are situated in Gardens and Fields. At the top of this Street is a Lane which leads to the West-gate, Quarry-house, &c. it borders upon a Field called the Shoulder of Mutton.

The History of Newcastle upon Tyne, Henry Bourne 1736

The word 'gate' in Gallow-gate is used in the sense of being the way or route to the gallows, there was never a physical gate called Gallowgate in the walls of Newcastle or on that road. Fortunately there is one map more than 200 years old stored in the archives of Northumberland Record Office which helps to sort out this problem. Gallowgate becomes Barrack Road. In the 18th century Barrack Road was the Turnpike Road and it was the main route out of Newcastle towards Cowgate, Ponteland and, to the north west, Northumberland and the borders.

Barrack Road acquired its name from the military barracks which were erected on the Town Moor and opened in 1806. To the right of Barrack Road today, where Leazes Park ends, is the old stone wall which surrounded the barracks in the 19th century. A little further along is the heavy stone gateway which marks the original entrance into the barracks. The old barracks gate has, for some years, been used as a public house. On the opposite side of the road are some residential buildings belonging to the Sutton's Trust, called Sutton's Dwellings. However, in the 18th century that was the site of an old stone quarry, the Gallowgate Quarry.

The survival of the plan is crucial to fixing the exact point of town gallows. The measurements quoted on the plan can be checked against modern maps and

Right, a map of 1764, showing the site of the gallows.

Northumberland Record Office

WANSPECK Turnpike Road

GROUND'S

West Cow Gate

Wanspeck Turnpike Road

W

E

S

MOOR

FENHAM

TOWN MOOR

ELSWICK GROUNDS

TOWN MOOR

TOWN MOOR

TOWN MOOR

TOWN

The Road made by the Corporation from Newcastle to Join the Wanspeck Turnpike Road

Quarries

Gallows

Leazes

New castle

A. *Fenham Gate and the 2 Lodges; a the Old Cottage; b The Ancient Gate;*
B. *The Ancient Carriage Roads from Newcastle to Fenham;*
C. *The French cut putting Cross the Ancient Road into the Joint C.P.*
D. *The Road marked out by a Committee of the Common Council in 1753 and never interrupted till February 1763.*
E. *The Water-course cross the Meetings of the Ancient Carriage Roads and the French Cut Cross the said Road*
D. *the remains of an Old Causeway appears to this day Cross the said Water-Courses.*
F. *An Ancient Gate from Fenham Grounds on to the Town Moor.*
North from the said Quarries at . . . to G the remains of an Old Causeway appears for about 20 Yards.
From the said Quarries North West . . . to Fenham boundary at Ancient Gate b is about 1154 yards.
North from the said Quarries along the Road made by the Corporation from Newcastle to join Wanspeck
Turnpike Road to the East end of the Road D marked out by the Committee of the Common Council about 984 Yards
North from the East end of the said Road D marked out by the Committee of the Common Council along the said Road
made by the Corporation from Newcastle to join Wanspeck Turnpike Road at the West Cow Gate about 1016 yards.

were accurately recorded. An image of the gallows appears on the map together with the word 'Gallows'. It is to the east of the Turnpike Road and the old quarry is shown on the west side of the road. Relating those points to modern maps shows that the Gallows Hole was on the boundary between the first part of the barracks of 1806 and an extension of 1877.

All of these facts drawn together show that the Gallows Hole was at a point now covered by the car park at the back of the office block of the Regional Blood Transfusion Service. It is on low ground in relation to the old turnpike road. The ground slopes away from the road and in the 18th century would have made a natural viewing area for the public executions that took place there.

Adjoining the moor near the old quarry in what became the Stanhope Street development there were field names North, Middle and South Gallows Flat (an old English word for a field).

Another confirmation is to be found in the maps of Northumberland published by Andrew Armstrong in 1769. In the map covering Newcastle upon Tyne the town gallows is clearly marked in the correct location but the scale is too small to place it with the same precision as the map described earlier.

As may be seen from the list of executions (page 115) there were 15 people hanged at the Gallows Hole in the 18th century. Those convicted of murder were hanged the next day but one after sentence. There was no appeal system.

These prisoners were kept in solitary confinement and fed on bread and water until executed. The bodies of murderers were either gibbeted in chains near the

This 1769 map by Andrew Armstrong clearly shows the gallows on the road north.

scene of their crimes or given over to the local surgeons for medical research which included the dissection of the body accompanied by public lectures.

Generally speaking, for other offenders sentenced to death there was a lapse of two to three weeks before execution. But for all condemned prisoners there was a procession from the prison at Newgate up Gallowgate to the gallows.

A procession always included a clergyman, the gaoler, the sheriff and the officers of the town, the prisoner manacled in a cart, and the hangman. Sometimes a coffin would also be taken to the gallows. In theory the objective was to make a public spectacle of the offender to give a grim reminder to spectators of the terrible retribution facing criminals. Certainly the public turned out in droves to be present at executions; they travelled to Newcastle from far and wide. But if the aim was to make it a solemn, moving, dignified demonstration of a community exacting the ultimate penalty for a grievous offence, it fell short of that objective.

Public executions became something of a carnival with people jostling for the best view. Drink was on sale with inevitable consequences. Occasionally it was just too much for some members of the public. On 21 August 1776 a postman named Robert Knowles was hanged on the Town Moor for stealing from the post, and the same day Andrew Mackenzie was executed for robbery at Westgate. A Newcastle butcher named William Robson wanted to witness both executions and, after hurrying between the two venues, dropped dead of a heart attack at Westgate.

Perhaps other events that day at the Gallows Hole were too much for Robson:

WEDNESDAY Robert Knowles was executed on the Town Moor for stealing a letter out of the Post-office here, containing two bank notes. He read his confession at the gallows with great composure, acknowledged the justness of his sentence and died very penitent.

At the execution of Knowles on Wednesday a little before he was turned off, a great uproar happened among the populace, which it is supposed took its rise from the ground on a old pit heap where people were standing giving way, and occasioned a sudden outcry, which startled some horses that ran among the crowd; in an instant the consternation became almost general, some flying one way and some another, without knowing for what reason; in the tumult many were thrown down and run over; but we hear of no material accident, further than some slight bruises, and the loss of hats, cloaks, shoes etc.

Newcastle Courant 24th August 1776

When the barracks site around the Gallows Hole was cleared and surveyed in the 1980s for the business park development, traces were found of old bell pits for coal. This seems to confirm the reference to an 'old pit heap.'

Knowles had been arrested in November the previous year, but he had not been prepared to sit quietly in Newgate Gaol awaiting his trial. He broke out of the gaol in June 1776 but his bid for freedom only lasted six days thanks to the work of some pitmen who were handsomely rewarded by Thomas Harle the Gaoler.

GENERAL HUE AND CRY, NEWCASTLE UPON TYNE June 1, 1776 BREACH of PRISON and ESCAPE

Whereas about nine o'clock this night, ROBERT KNOWLES, a prisoner in His Majesty's Gaol in this town, for feloniously stealing and taking a Post-letter and two Bank of England Notes inclosed therein, from out of the Public Post-office in the said town, broke out of the said gaol and escaped: He appears about thirty years of age, four feet eleven inches high, somewhat round shouldered, has black hair clubbed behind, is of swarthy complexion, a little pock-marked, and has a large cut on his upper lip, his legs somewhat crooked, and had on light-coloured cloaths when he escaped.

Whoever shall apprehend the said Robert Knowles, and lodge him in any of his Majesty's gaols or deliver him to the Gaoler of Newcastle shall be paid a reward of TWENTY GUINEAS over and above all reasonable charges, by THOMAS HARLE; Gaoler.

Newcastle Courant Saturday June 8th, 1776

There were many dextrous pickpockets in the North East in the 18th century and they were often active amongst the crowds at executions. The pressure in the crowds, the excitement and the distraction of the moment of execution must have been a golden opportunity for them. In 1783 the proprietors of the *Newcastle Courant* felt it was time to inform their readers about the methods used by pickpockets and how to deal with them:

A CAUTION against PICK-POCKETS and SHOP-LIFTERS,

Intended to draw the attention of the public to the means of prevention or detection.

There are generally two sometimes three persons concerned in picking a Pocket: their game is in a crowd, they resort to all Fairs, Horse Races, Cock-Pits, Playhouses &c. and they don't there appear to be connected with or even know each other: Their first step is to single out the person on whom the attempt is to be made, which they do by secret signs and motions, this being done Ambidexter contrives to place himself at the Pocket-side of the person, an accomplice then gets close up to his other side, and if there is a third in the plot, he moves close up behind Ambidexter, and whilst Amby is exercising his dexterity at the Pocket, his accomplice on the person's other side by justling him or some other artful manoeuvre, endeavouring to draw his attention from his pocket-side: If Amby succeeds he instantly delivers the booty to the third person, who quickly marches off with it; but if there is not a third, then Amby speedily moves off with what he has got.

Newcastle Courant 7th June 1783

Such pickpockets were prepared to try their luck even underneath the gallows:

Wednesday [i.e. 30th August 1786] Henry Jennings was executed on the Town Moor, pursuant to his sentence at the last Assizes for Horse-stealing whilst he was hanging on the Gallows, one Thomas Brown, Millwright, standing almost directly under it, had his right side pocket picked of 6s 6d and in two or three minutes afterwards one Thomas Hamilton, Cordwainer, standing very near the gallows, detected one Andrew Donaldson, Glover and Breeches maker, with his hand in the said Hamilton's Breeches pocket, on which Hamilton procured a Constable and carried him before the Mayor.

Newcastle Courant Saturday 2nd September 1786

The arrival at the gallows of the procession from the gaol heightened the mood and expectation of the crowd. Prayers and speeches followed with much effort by the chaplains at the gaol and other clergymen to make criminals repent. Reports on executions invariably included the words 'the prisoner died penitent.'

The prayers were followed by the final speech by the prisoner if he wished, or felt able, to speak. There is quite strong evidence that the prisoners were given substantial help by the clergy in preparing their final speeches. What examples survive are often expressed in the language of an educated man and few of the condemned prisoners fell into that category. The speeches also included many exhortations to the Almighty for forgiveness and mercy. Speeches could run to more than 1,500 words and combine confession, a sermon on the temptations of earthly life and the need for repentance, and thanks for the humanity and consideration shown to the prisoner by various officials and individuals.

In 1783 there were two chaplains charged with the spiritual care of the prisoners at Newgate Gaol. One was John Brown, Curate at St John's Parish Church, the other was the famous Newcastle historian, John Brand, Curate at St Andrew's Church. The chaplains were each paid £10 per annum for their work at the gaol.

The pastoral care of condemned prisoners was not left just to the chaplains. The itinerant preachers, John and Charles Wesley, frequently visited Newgate Gaol as part of their Methodist mission. Charles Wesley, for example, took a close interest in a man charged with kicking his teenage daughter downstairs to her death. Richard Brown was a keelman from Sandgate and he was sentence to be hanged for the crime, committed on 10th November, 1750.

There seems to have been a mixture of morbid public curiosity and sympathy for Richard Brown. The young apprentice hostman, Ralph Jackson, recorded in his journal a visit to Newgate Gaol to see Brown. Jackson's master, William Jefferson, employed many keelmen and, as a charitable gesture, sent sixpence for Brown.

Charles Wesley spent a great deal of time with Brown, but claimed, 'Never have I spoken to a more hardened, ignorant, stupid sinner. He utterly denied the fact. I prayed for him with little hope.'

After many visits and many prayers, Wesley grew to have some influence on Brown, and on the morning of the execution Brown was described as quite calm and resigned showing all the marks of repentance and faith in death. In his dying speech, Brown alleged 'he had no Intention to take away [his daughter's] Life, and that he was so much inebriated at the Time he perpetrated this horrid Scene, that he could not recollect the several barbarous Circumstances with which he was charged'.

The gallows was simply constructed of two sturdy upright posts set firmly in the ground with a beam across the top. Brief entries in local records in 1616 show the resourceful authorities at Newcastle making use of half a ship's mast and two trees to replace the Town Moor Gallows at a cost of 37s 6d.

In the 18th century hanging was a crude process. There were no refinements, such as a trap door that would provide a drop to break the neck of the condemned man or woman. The hangman strapped the hands and arms of the prisoner to prevent any attempt to escape or interfere with the execution. The rope was fastened to the crossbar with a noose at the other end. A ladder was put against the cross bar and the prisoner was required to mount the ladder. The executioner followed and fixed the noose around the neck of the condemned. He then returned to the bottom of the ladder and turned it so that the prisoner swung under the gallows hanging from the rope. Hence the expression 'turned off' that appeared in so many of the press reports on executions. The effect of this process was death by strangulation, which could be long and painful. The body of the prisoner was left hanging for at least one hour and checked for signs of life before being taken down.

There are many examples of executed criminals reviving even after hanging for an hour or more on the gallows. A famous local legend relates to Ewen Macdonald hanged at Newcastle upon Tyne in 1752 for murder whose remarkable story is explored on page 102.

If there was no court order for the body to be gibbeted or passed to the surgeons for dissection, the body would simply be handed over to the next of kin or friends for burial. There was no objection to executed criminals being buried in church grave yards in hallowed ground. There are numerous examples in the burial registers of the principal parish churches of Newcastle. However it was usual to bury criminals on the north side of the church where the grave would be forever in the shadow of the church building and not touched by the sun. People who committed suicide, on the other hand, would not be allowed a grave in a churchyard but instead would be buried at the crossroads out of town with a wooden stake driven through the heart. This custom was abolished in 1823.

It was common for broad-sheets about executions to be published. Often as not they were based on information supplied by the clergy attending the condemned criminals. In 1795 Thomas Purvis of Newcastle became involved in settling an argument at a beer tent at Newcastle races about payment for beer between patrons and a serving woman. The gang concerned were angry about the outcome and lay in wait for Purvis outside the race course. Nine or ten men attacked him, and he died of his wounds. The gang fled from the town but within a few days the authorities were rounding them up. Thomas Nicholson the chief suspect was arrested at Berwick on Tweed and brought down to Newgate Gaol and later sentenced to death.

The broad-sheet published after the execution of Thomas Nicholson is typical of its kind:

A PARTICULAR ACCOUNT OF THOMAS NICHOLSON, A PITMAN

Who was executed at Tyburn, near Newcastle upon Tyne, on Saturday, 8th August 1795, pursuant to his sentence, for the Murder of THOMAS PURVIS, Carver and Guilder.

Thomas Nicholson was in the 23rd year of his age, by trade a Pitman, and late employed in the Bigg's Main Colliery. On Saturday afternoon, before Newcastle Race Week, he went with his brother, John Nicholson, to the Town Moor, where they accidentally fell in company with a number of their acquaintances, at a Public Tent, on the Race-ground, and joined them in drinking and social

conversation. On calling the reckoning, some difference arose between the company and the girl who attended, respecting the number of Pints they had drank; and, she supposing herself likely to be wronged by them, requested Mr Purvis (who happened to be in the same Tent) to assist her in adjusting the dispute, which he humanely accomplished; but not in a manner agreeable to the expectations of Thomas Nicholson or his comrades, who all vowed revenge against him. Accordingly they watched his coming off the moor, and finding him without a guardian friend most cruelly beat and mangled his body; leaving him apparently dead, in which melancholy condition he was taken up by some gentlemen, accidentally passing that way, and conveyed to his house in Pilgrimstreet, where he languished, in the most agonizing torture, until the Saturday following, when the hand of death, more merciful than savage murderers, relieved him from his mortal misery.

Thomas Nicholson, being with four others of the assassins apprehended and tried at the Assizes, he was convicted of having acted the most cruelly in this barbarous tragical scene; and consequently condemned to be hanged, and his body delivered to the surgeons for dissection, according to act of parliament.

His relations having liberty to visit him in the Prison at Newgate; on Friday, his parting with a Father, Brother, and Sister, was remarkably tender and moving; the complicated struggle of sorrow and affection, touched the compassionate feelings of every person who saw them. At the place of execution, he could not sum up the fortitude to utter any formal speech, but appeared to have an adequate just sense of the heinousness of his crime; and it is hoped his just punishment will make a proper serious impression upon those of his guilty accomplices, and all other SABBATH-BREAKERS of every description.

Thomas Nicholson was the last condemned prisoner to be hanged at the Gallows Hole. After the building of the first part of the barracks in 1806, the site for executions was moved further along the old turnpike road and to the west, probably about opposite where the BBC Broadcasting Centre stands today. There is a gentle slope upwards to the west at that point and it would have provided a grandstand view for the public to watch executions.

When Newcastle upon Tyne was created a town and county in its own right by royal charter in 1400 the Castlegarth around the Keep remained county land. The county of Northumberland surrounded the walls of Newcastle upon Tyne and also the upper part of the town now known as the Haymarket, Spital Tongues and the Town Moor. That remained the position for more than 400 years until the Municipal Corporations Act of 1835 extended the town boundaries of Newcastle to include Byker, Heaton, Jesmond, Westgate and Elswick.

The St John's parish church burial records for Newcastle reveal that Northumberland county executions in the 17th century took place within Castlegarth at what was referred to as the 'Hye Castle.' There are no records of executions in Castlegarth after the 17th century. However the county authorities kept the option open even in the 19th century. A new Moot Hall for Northumberland was erected in Castlegarth between 1810 and 1812 and the Act of Parliament of 1809, permitting the raising of funds for the building of the Moot Hall, included a section authorising the Sheriff of Northumberland to erect a gallows and hang criminals in Castlegarth.

In the 18th century the executions for Northumberland were carried out either at Morpeth or outside the Westgate at Newcastle upon Tyne. As an ordinary matter of routine for prisoners sentenced to death, the gaoler would take the prisoners back to Morpeth Gaol and the execution would follow two or three weeks later. The 1750 Act requiring people convicted of murder to be executed the next day but one after sentence has already been mentioned. The impact of this law on Northumberland executions meant that the authorities needed a gallows at or near Newcastle for criminals convicted of murder as there was insufficient time to take such prisoners back to Morpeth and have them executed quickly. The Westgate gallows served the purpose and were occasionally used for other offenders. During the 18th century 12 Northumberland criminals were hanged at Westgate; six for mur-

The West Gate in the town wall; it stood where Westgate Road meets Bath Lane. Northumberland executions were carried out at the gallows here.

der, two for coining and one each for horse-stealing, house-breaking, returning
from transportation and robbery.

Condemned prisoners were held in the dungeon at the Keep then brought in
procession along Bailiff Gate opposite Black Gate and along Westgate Street until
they reached the West Gate in the town walls, where the party passed out of
Newcastle and into Northumberland. Isaac Thompson's map of Newcastle upon
Tyne dated 1746 fixes the exact point of the Northumberland county gallows as the
bottom of Back (Bath) Lane where it joined Westgate Street (now Westgate Road).

The fact that Thompson marked the county gallows on his map suggests it was
regarded as a permanent fixture. Two years before the map was published, the
Northumberland authorities had paid £15 7s to Edward Stuart, the Under Sheriff of

The Keep in the late 18th century, from Mackenzie's History of Newcastle upon Tyne.

Northumberland, for a gallows to be erected there to hang Maben, Samuel and Lister, two coiners, and a horse thief.

The last prisoner to be hanged outside the Westgate was Thomas Clare, a young soldier from Staffordshire, hanged on Friday August 16th, 1805. Clare robbed and murdered a pitman named William Todd, who he found in a field near the military camp, sleeping off the effects of a heavy drinking session. The broadsheet describes his crime:

> On Sunday morning 19th August 1804, between three and four o'clock, as two Drummers and a Private belonging to the Staffordshire Militia, were gathering Mushrooms in a field near Cullercoats, they were alarmed by the cries of a person in distress; they then made towards the place, on entering the second field, they perceived a man's hat. One of them took it up and said it was Thomas Clare's. Almost instantly as he expressed those words a Soldier jumped over the hedge, and ran towards the Camps. They had not proceeded above twenty yards farther when they observed the body of a man laying in the Ditch, almost double; they instantly supposed he had been murdered by the Person then making his escape. As soon as they arrived at the Camps, they gave information to the Sergeant of the company to which Clare belonged, and he was directly taken in his tent, and sent to the Guard.
>
> There was a piece of rail found near the body of the deceased, partly covered with blood, with which it appear'd the horrid deed had been committed; his face was much bruised, and a large wound just above the left eye; one arm and some of his ribs were broken, and several black marks on his body; he appear'd to be about 50 years of age; and has left a widow and seven children.
>
> The above unfortunate culprit was born at Tunstall, in Staffordshire, was about 23 years of age, and a stout healthy looking young man. Since his sentence he behaved in a becoming manner, was very penitent, and seemed sensible of his approaching dissolution.

The county gallows remained on the site until the Westgate was demolished in 1811. That redevelopment, combined with the provision of a new gaol at Morpeth in 1828 and the expansion of Newcastle in 1835, put an end to executions of

Northumberland county criminals at Newcastle until the Morpeth Gaol closed 1881.

A gallows should not be confused with a gibbet. The gallows was usually at a fixed location in reach of the prison, and was the place of execution. A gibbet, on the other hand, was a sturdy upright post with a diagonal support for a short horizontal bar on top from which the body was hung after death. The offender, usually a murderer, was executed at the county or town gallows, then the body was covered with pitch, encased in a bag of chains or metal straps and suspended on the gibbet near the scene of the crime as a grim warning to others. The body was left to rot which could take many years. The practice of gibbeting offenders was formally ended on 25th July 1834.

Not all prisoners condemned to death were actually hanged. Many were reprieved for transportation and occasionally, in special circumstances, a full pardon would be granted.

There were times when the judges seemed inflexible and unwilling to use their power to reprieve offenders sentenced to death and transport them overseas instead. Take the case of Alice Williamson, 'an aged offender' hanged on the Town Moor at Newcastle upon Tyne on 7th August 1758 'for feloniously and burglariously breaking into the dwelling-house of Robert Marshall and stealing several goods.' Robert Marshall was a Newcastle baker. He owned a house in Middle Street, which was opposite St Nicholas' Church between the Groat Market and the Flesh Market (now called Cloth Market). He also had another house, which appears to have included a shop, in the Groat Market.

Marshall and a companion named Elizabeth Landirth caught Alice Williamson, red-handed, at midnight on Friday 14th April 1758, stealing clothing and household linen from Marshall's house in the Groat Market. Williamson was tried and convicted of the capital offence. This woman, described as 'an aged offender' – she may have been as old as 68 years – was sentenced to death by hanging.

The last public execution at Newcastle took place on 14th March 1863 when George Vass aged 19 years was hanged at the Carliol Square Gaol for the murder of Margaret Jane Docherty at West Walls, Newcastle. The authorities put a gallows on top of the south-west corner of the gaol, not far from the back entrance to the Royal Arcade leading through to Pilgrim Street. Vass was hanged by Thomas

The Bigg Market in the early 19th century. The Groat Market Market lies beyond.

Askern. There is an eye-witness account left to us by Archibald Reed in a book called *Bruce's School* published in 1908:

> This wretched spectacle was performed for the last time on the very spot where the fair was held (i.e. in Carliol Square around the gaol). In the early sixties a man named Vass was tried and condemned to death for the murder and outrage of an old woman near the 'West Walls'. The whole length of the street from the Arcade steps to Carliol Street was barricaded strongly at very short intervals, forming pens, to avoid accidents through the enormous crowds anticipated, and well it was so, for every available space was filled. The writer viewed the situation from the roof of a house immediately opposite the scaffold, which was erected on top of the gaol wall on the south-west corner opposite the railway bank that leads to Pilgrim Street; and looking down as far as the eye could carry, the whole thoroughfare had the appearance of a street paved with human heads. These people assembled as early as 5.30am. By 8 o'clock the crowd was so dense that dozens of people had fainted; and these were passed over the heads of the multitude to the outside. The story of the execution is soon told; the condemned man was under a minute in view before he disappeared from the gaze of the bloodthirsty mob.

3 Stand and Deliver!

As very few, if any, of the highwaymen who come upon the roads near this town escape being taken so we hope these novices* will soon share the same fate, there being a sharp lookout after them; in the mean time we recommend it to travellers, to carry as little money or other valuable effects with them as possible, and always to be provided with such weapons as are best adapted to their own use, and with good courage, for one honest man with a good heart will vanquish several villains.

Newcastle Courant Saturday 23rd October 1790

(*a highway robbery near Gosforth)

In the 18th century, travelling the roads of the North East alone, particularly at night, could be very dangerous. Cries for help could lead the unwary traveller into deep trouble. Usually there was no subterfuge or subtlety about robbery on the highways.

The term 'highwayman' seems to have been applied to the highway thief using a horse as distinguished from the 'foot-pad' working on foot, but there was nothing romantic about the so-called 'Gentlemen of the Road.' The average foot-pad or mounted robber was neither gentle nor courteous. Some highwaymen did become nationally notorious and revered by their own kind, but their romantic image was a myth created by literature and Hollywood. The use of firearms was commonplace amongst these criminals. They were the muggers of their day.

Some footpads and highwaymen even attacked their victims within sight of the town gallows at Newcastle. It seemed that the prospect of hanging was not actually a deterrent for criminals.

That night (i.e. Saturday last) as a gentleman, who lives at Whalton, was riding home, on the Ponteland Turnpike, two men armed with pistols, came out of the quarries near the gallows, and bid him stand; upon which they cut the horses bridle and saddle girth, and one held a pistol to his breast, whilst the other rifled his waist-coat pocket of a tobacco box; and being told they would get nothing more, they struck him on the head with such violence, that he fell to the ground; they then robbed him of his money, and made their escape; but he recovered soon after, walked back to town, his horse having left him.

Newcastle Journal, Saturday 14th February 1767

It is also a myth that highwaymen treated their female victims with courtesy, if not a little flirtation. Both men and women were brutally attacked.

Tuesday about six in the evening, a woman from Elsdon, coming to this town to buy goods, was attacked on the Moor near the Gallows, by two fellows, who knocked her down and robbed her of 60 guineas and £6 in bank notes, which were sewed up in her petticoats.

Newcastle Courant Saturday 10th August 1776

Tuesday morning about 5 o'clock as a butcher of this town was riding along the Town Moor, a man upon horseback attempted to stop his horse near the gallows; on which he rode off with all speed; and when further along the road, a fellow levelled a stick at his head, which fortunately hit only the horse behind the saddle. Presently, after he heard the fellow on horseback coming up in full gallop, he prudently rode of the road, till he heard him go past; on which he returned to the town.

Newcastle Courant Saturday 8th November 1783

The Hue and Cry column of the *Newcastle Courant* helped the authorities to catch offenders. This initiative was established in the autumn of 1772 when Sir John Fielding, the blind Chief Metropolitan Magistrate, wrote to all the clerks of the peace around the country proposing to the justices that the local newspaper should carry a GENERAL HUE AND CRY column on the front page. It would include details of crimes, suspects and wanted persons sent out from Bow Street Police Office in London under Fielding's supervision. To this information would be added details of local crimes. Before this there had only been piecemeal coverage on the news

A depiction of the famous highwayman Dick Turpin from a 19th-century account: The Chronicles of Crime *by Camden Pelham, 1886.*

pages and some criminals moving about the country may not have had their activities reported at all. The idea was well received and taken up at once by the *Newcastle Courant*. The Hue and Cry was not printed in other newspapers although they would carry news reports of crimes and so on. The first General Hue and Cry appeared in the *Newcastle Courant* on Saturday 5th December 1772. It contained information from Bow Street on three prison escapees at Hertfordshire, another from Leicester and descriptions of five horses stolen from various places in the south of England. Northumberland published details of seven vagrants held at the county gaol in Morpeth, descriptions of two footpads who robbed William Atkinson of cash on the highway at Glanton near Whittingham. The Newcastle authorities published details of an alleged murder of a 'new born Male child' found buried at East Ballast Hills and descriptions of two Rogues and Vagabonds now held in the House of Correction.

Early in 1783 a robbery had taken place a few hundred yards north of the town gallows on the lane leading into Fenham from the turnpike road out of Newcastle to Ponteland and beyond. That quiet lane to Fenham is now Fenham Hall Drive.

GENERAL HUE AND CRY
COUNTY of NORTHUMBERLAND

A ROBBERY – REWARDS for a DISCOVERY 5th August 1783

On Saturday night last about nine o'clock, George Shaw, Farmer, was attacked in the Lane leading from the Town Moor to Fenham and robbed of a Leg of Veal which he was bringing from Newcastle market. The robber wounded him desperately in the forehead with a Strickle or Scythe Sharpener, and left him senseless on the road. The person robbed is not able to give any description of the Robber. Any person or persons discovering the Offender or offenders shall receive a reward of Ten Guineas on his or their conviction, to be paid by William Ord, of Fenham Esq. over and above the reward of Forty Pounds given by Act of Parliament.

Newcastle Courant Saturday 6th September 1783

1783 seems to have been an active year for highway robbery. In November the local news on the back page of the *Newcastle Courant* and the Hue and Cry on the front page were packed full of news about one robbery, an attempted robbery on the Town Moor by two foot pads, and the arrest of Sylvannus Broadwater for robbery. There was also an example of the current strategy for obtaining information and evidence about robbers by offering rewards and pardons to criminals for informing on their partners and turning 'King's Evidence' as it was called.

Newcastle Courant Saturday 22nd November 1783

Last Tuesday afternoon (18th November) two foot pads committed a robbery upon the North Road on the Moor of this town … and attempted another robbery the same afternoon upon the West Turnpike Road on the same Moor; but the Gentleman they attacked there, by striking one of them (who had seized hold of his horses bridle) a blow with the but-end of his whip, on the shoulder which was aimed at his head, and clapping spurs to his horse, happily extracted himself from him; the other immediately fired a pistol after

Even in 1905 when this photograph was taken, Fenham Hall Drive, next to Newcastle's Town Moor, was a lonely and vulnerable road.

him but providentially missed him: we have not the least doubt of these two Highwaymen being soon taken and brought to exemplary punishment, as there are tolerable good grounds to suspect who they are; (let those who harbour them hearken to that) and a sharp look out is after them, upon a secret plan, that can hardly fail of detecting and securing them. They have certainly mistaken their place, they are too near Newcastle; justice is at their heels, vengeance lies in wait for them. In the mean time we recommend it to all persons to avoid travelling too late in the afternoon, and to carry no bills, and as little money or other valuable property about them as possible.

NEWCASTLE November 20th 1783

HIGHWAY ROBBERY – REWARDS for a DISCOVERY

Whereas Jasper Anderson of Coxlodge near this town, Farmer, was, about half past six o'clock on Tuesday evening last, the 18th instant, attacked upon the North Post Road on the Moor of this town, near the Cross Causeway leading to Haddricks Mill by two FOOT PADS, who seized his horse by the bridle on each side, beat him desperately on the head with their sticks, and robbed him of an Edinburgh Guinea Bank Note, a PROMISSORY NOTE dated in the year

1785 for payment of NINE POUNDS to Jasper Anderson or Order, forty days after date and signed Joseph Story, a small Pocket book with black slate leaves, a very considerable sum in gold and silver, among which was a half sovereign of base metal silvered. One of them left on the spot a remarkable thorn walking stick, which may be seen in the hands of John Young Sergeant at Mace.

One of these highwaymen appeared to be tall and stout made and had on a coarse jacket and no coat; The other was a middle sized broad made man, in a light coloured brown jacket, and they both had round hats.

Who ever will discover the said offenders, so as they, or either of them, by that means be taken and convicted, shall thereupon, (over and above the reward of FORTY POUNDS given by Act of Parliament, to be paid by the Sheriff, and an exemption from Ward and Parish Offices) be entitled to the further rewards of TWENTY POUNDS, to be paid by the Town Clerk, and FIVE GUINEAS to be paid by the said Jasper Anderson.

And if either of the said offenders, before he is taken, will, voluntarily before a Magistrate of this Town, discover his accomplice, so as such accomplice be by that means convicted, such DISCOVERER shall thereupon, not only have the two afore-mentioned rewards, but endeavours shall be used to procure him his Majesty's pardon.

If therefore either of the said offenders be desirous of leaving off his dangerous course of life, reforming and saving himself, let him lose no time in making the discovery, less his partner as well as for the sake of the Rewards, as to save his own neck, should slip in before him and make the Discovery, and turn King's Evidence.

The robbers were James Chambers and William Collins alias Nicholson. They were arrested on Sunday 11th January 1784, on suspicion of robbing Jasper Anderson. They were also suspected of robbing John Kell near Stamfordham in Northumberland in November 1783. However Chambers and Collins were actually indicted for the Anderson robbery and detained in Newgate Gaol until their trial. They were both sentenced to hang, and it is said the two robbers were afterwards buried in the same grave in St Andrew's Churchyard.

Being convicted of highway robbery did not mean automatic execution. Sylvannus Broadwater was tried at the Northumberland Assizes for robbing Patrick Wallace of a pocket book and other things in the parish of Low Edlingham on 17th October 1783. Broadwater was found guilty and sentenced to death, but the judge reprieved him for transportation. Broadwater did not learn the lessons of his experiences. He was not actually transported across the seas because of the effect of the

American War of Independence, but held on prison hulks in the south of England. On 21st September 1791, Broadwater and a man called Joseph Marshall were arrested for stealing two horses.

> **Wednesday (i.e. September 21st) Sylvester Broadwater and Joseph Marshall two old offenders were committed to Morpeth Gaol for stealing two horses left upon Mickley Bank as advertised in our last Hue and Cry.**
>
> *Newcastle Courant* 24th September 1791.

This time he was variously recorded as Sylvannus or Sylvester Broadwater. The writing was on the wall for Broadwater and Marshall, they were tried at the Northumberland Assizes in August 1792, convicted and sentenced to death. There was no reprieve this time. Broadwater, and Marshall, together with Christopher Taylor condemned for arson and robbery at Bardon Mill, were hanged together in a triple execution at Morpeth on Wednesday 22nd August 1792.

In 1776 two soldiers, Andrew McKenzie and Barney Rea, from the 70th Regiment of Foot, robbed a traveller on the Shields Road from Newcastle. They were arrested on the same night, but two nights later the Irish prisoner, Rea, made an audacious, and probably nauseating, escape by climbing down the privy. The Hue and Cry notice for Barney Rea was reprinted from January to the end of March but he was not seen again.

> ### GENERAL HUE AND CRY
>
> COUNTY OF NORTHUMBERLAND. **Escaped from Justice Barney Rea, a private soldier in 70th regiment of foot, now lying in Newcastle, about five foot five inches and a half high, thick made large grey eyes, dark brown hair rather too short for tying behind, born in Queen's County Ireland. Had on when he escaped a regimental coat, white waistcoat edged red, white breeches and stockings. He is strongly suspected of having been guilty of committing an assault and robbery on the King's Highway, leading from Shields to Newcastle upon Tyne. – Any person apprehending him will be entitled to a reward of Forty Pounds on conviction.**
>
> *Newcastle Courant* Saturday 23rd March 1776

His accomplice, McKenzie, was left to face the county hangman after trial at the Northumberland Assizes in August 1776. According to newspaper reports, McKenzie showed great contrition after sentencing. He intended speaking at the gallows, but before he had managed to deliver two lines, his spirits failed him.

Finally there is the story of Joseph Hall a soldier hanged in 1765 for highway robbery at Gosforth.

On Tuesday 11th September, 1764, at about eight o'clock in the evening, William Cuthbertson, a haircutter, was returning to Newcastle from Morpeth in a post-chaise. A little beyond the Three Mile Bridge, a footpad fired his pistol at the driver, whose face was badly burned in the attack. The horses took fright and dragged the post-chaise away from the attacker. The footpad then attacked two more travellers, but his pistol misfired and they were able to escape. In the meantime Cuthbertson had arrived at the Three Mile Bridge and raised the alarm. The footpad was soon apprehended. He proved to be a soldier, Joseph Hall, wearing his uniform which he had turned inside out. Pistols and ammunition were found in his pockets. He readily confessed his guilt.

Joseph Hall appeared at the Northumberland Assizes before Sir Joseph Yates Knight, Thursday morning 8th August 1765. He was charged with 'feloniously shooting at Thomas Wanless at the Parish of Gosforth in the King's Highway with a pistol loaded with powder and Ball.' Hall was found guilty and sentenced to be hanged.

4 Gaols and Gaolers

Northern Circuit NORTHUMBERLAND

Assize held at Newcastle, whither prisoners are conveyed; and men and women confined together seven or eight nights in a dirty damp dungeon down six steps in the old castle, which having no roof, in a wet season the water is some inches deep. The felons are chained to rings in the wall.

The State of the Prisons in England and Wales By John Howard

The Keep

Northumberland only used the basement of the ruined Keep for a few days once a year for prisoners appearing at the Northumberland Assize court and at the county Quarter Sessions, but conditions in the gaol were quite desperate. They reveal much about what 18th century society thought acceptable for prisoners. To add to the degradation Howard also informs us that on Assize Sunday members of the public could, on payment of sixpence, be admitted to the gaol to view the prisoners.

Simple confinement in a closed building was not widely used as a punishment in the North East in the 18th century. An analysis of ten per cent of Newcastle upon Tyne and Northumberland Assize Court sentences and other findings includes no sentence of imprisonment. Local custodial sentences, particularly at the quarter sessions, were much more likely to involve the House of Correction rather than the ordinary or common gaol.

The provincial prisons of that time served three basic purposes. First to hold prisoners waiting for trial; second, to hold prisoners until their sentence – usually death or transportation – came into effect; and thirdly, debtor prisoners, who represented a large part of gaoler's responsibilities and income.

The effect of this practice was that prisoners often spent very long periods in gaol because the local Assizes were held just once a year, usually at the beginning of August. A person charged and committed to gaol early in September faced a long wait in discomfort for trial nearly twelve months later. Then there were other quirks in the system. If a criminal was sentenced to death and reprieved by the judges for transportation, he usually waited in gaol for the pardon to come through, then for sentence of transportation to be confirmed at the next Assizes twelve months later. Such a prisoner could have spent the best part of two years in prison by the time of final sentence. Clearing prisoners out of the North East gaols to the convict ships was an erratic business, dependant on numbers and other factors, and took place in the late autumn or often into the winter which meant more time spent in gaol. So in reality, guilty or not, sentenced or not, prisoners were spending many, many months in custody, and there was no indication the courts ever took that into account.

On commitment to gaol, each prisoner was required to pay a sum of money to the gaoler, and on discharge a further, larger sum. At Newgate prison in Newcastle

Newgate Prison from the south.

the discharge fees were 13s 4d to the gaoler and one shilling to the turnkey. The fees applied whether the prisoner was found guilty or innocent, and many prisoners spent longer in gaol than necessary because they did not have the money to pay their fees. The system was not abolished until 1815. In addition, newcomers to many gaols found their fellow prisoners demanding 'garnish'. This would probably be money, or if the new inmate was poor, some of their clothing. John Howard pointed out that prisoners deprived of clothing in freezing cold gaols were more prone to illnesses. Sometimes this proved fatal. Gaolers often turned a blind eye to the custom of demanding garnish. This was probably because the prisoners used the money to buy liquor, and the person supplying the liquor was usually the gaoler himself.

The authorities needed gaols and lock-ups of more than one description. At the commonest parish level was the village lock-up, used to confine drunks, disorderly people, vagrants and other nuisances. Usually this was the simplest of secure stone buildings seen as a temporary lock-up for such prisoners.

The Town Lock-up

The 'Tower of the Bridge', sometimes called the 'Tower on the Bridge' was Newcastle's equivalent of a village lock-up, albeit on a larger scale. It was somewhere to hold drunks and other nuisance offenders and also the suspects for more serious offences until they could be brought before the Mayor's Court for examination by magistrates. The Mayor of Newcastle was also the Chief Magistrate.

The 'Tower on the Bridge' is in the centre of this 1745 engraving by Buck.

There were three towers on the 13th century medieval stone bridge; the first, at the entrance on the Newcastle end, served the town as a magazine; there was another tower at the Gateshead end of the bridge; then near the middle was the tower serving Newcastle as a small gaol. How long it had been a gaol is not clear but this bridge tower gaol had a resident gaoler. In 1697 the Chamberlain's Account Books note payment to William Heslop of 20 shillings for the half year for 'taking care of ye prisoners'.

The bridge tower gaol was sometimes used to hold prisoners for the Northumberland justices until an escort to Morpeth Gaol could be arranged, but many of the tower's inmates were the vagabonds, petty thieves, prostitutes and shoplifters who made an illegal living on the streets of Newcastle.

Occasionally, a spell in the tower could produce extraordinary results, like the story of this vagabond, whose speech was mysteriously restored:

> On Saturday last a Person who appeared to be a Vagabond was detected begging in the Market here by Alderman Clayton, who order'd him to be confin'd 'till Monday, when upon Examination he pretended to have his Tongue cut out by the Turks; but on being order'd to the House of Correction, and threatened with hard Labour, he thought proper to speak; he says his name is William Robinson, was born at Jamaica, and has followed the Employment of a Pedlar in the South Country some time; upon which he was sent back to the House of Correction.
>
> *Newcastle Courant* Saturday 28th May 1748

At least one prisoner risked her life trying to escape.

> On Tuesday evening (25th September) a Woman confined in the Tower on the Bridge, who had been committed to Prison for Misdemeanours some Time before, being dissatisfied with her Lodgings, and having by some Means got her Irons off; crept out at one of the high Windows, through a place not above seven inches in diameter, and leapt into the River, to the surface of which was about twenty yards, What is very extraordinary, she was taken up by a Boat about forty Yards below, without having the least Damage, save a cold Bathing, &c. She is said to be disordered in her Senses, and was observed by several Spectators on the Bridge to swim in a methodical Manner, most of the Time she was in the Water.
>
> *Newcastle Journal* Saturday 30th September 1752

Petty criminals were held in the bridge tower gaol until they could be examined by a magistrate at the Mayor's Court in the Guildhall then brought to trial at the Quarter Sessions. Late in the 18th century a 'Sessions House' in the Manors was used for Quarter Sessions prisoners. Those prisoners charged with more serious offences were transferred to Newgate Gaol for trial at the Newcastle Assizes.

The three courts, Mayor's, Quarter Sessions and Assize all sat in the Guildhall courtroom. Occasionally the magistrates would use the bridge tower gaol as a marker for offenders to be whipped through the streets of the town. The Quarter Sessions Order Book for 1743-1777 notes at Christmas 1745-46 'Ann Willis, stealing silver beaker from Thomas Grey to be publickly whipt from Newgate to the Tower on the Bridge.' (See Chapter 5)

There were only a few years left in the life of the bridge tower gaol. Much of the bridge was swept away in the great floods of mid-November 1771. Everything including the old bridge tower gaol was demolished in the next two or three years and a new stone bridge was erected on the same site and opened to traffic on 30th April 1781.

To replace the bridge tower gaol the Newcastle upon Tyne authorities decided to use Close Gate one of the ancient gates in the town walls. Close Gate was to the west of the Mansion House and about two to three hundred yards from the

The town walls near Close Gate in 1882

Guildhall Court. More is known about this small prison because it was described by John Howard. It was the most basic of prisons, with no water or sewer and no yard to walk in for fresh air, a very uncomfortable place to be incarcerated. The gaoler's salary had risen to £10 per annum and he was entitled to fees of one shilling per prisoner, which seems high for what was probably a very short stay. Howard remarks that 'criminals are first committed to the Tower in the Close for a day or two, and if not discharged by a magistrate, are removed … to other prisons.'

John Howard paid four visits to the Tower in the Close. He found two prisoners in the gaol on two of those visits and one on each of the others, so it was by no means a busy prison.

Close Gate was demolished in 1797. The authorities then used the house of correction in the Manors as the overnight lock-up until it was decided to resume use of the Keep (by this time owned by Newcastle Corporation) as a gaol. It was only a stop-gap arrangement because there were plans for a new combined gaol and house of correction in Carliol Square.

The House of Correction

Just below Carliol Square, to the south, is the district called Manors. The land once belonged to an Augustine Monastery called St Austin Fryers, but was renamed King's Manor after the dissolution. Of the old public buildings in Manors, only the Holy Jesus Hospital, dating from 1682, has survived the developers. Clustered around it in the 18th century, however, were the Bridewell or House of Correction, a charity school, a workhouse and the Barber Surgeons' Hall. Later in that century there was a Sessions House amongst these buildings which was a gaol for holding prisoners awaiting trial at the Quarter Sessions.

According to John Brand, the butchers' company converted part of the old monastery into a tallow house (a building used for processing animal fat to make tallow for candles, soap etc.). John Howard, inspecting the gaols at about the same time, reported on two establishments at the Manors, first the 'Old House of Correction, called the Tallow House', to which prisoners were taken from the Tower in the Close. This was the building where prisoners for trial at the Quarter Sessions were held, and later in the century known as the Sessions House. Secondly, Howard visited the Bridewell (i.e. the House of Correction), describing 'two rooms, one for men, the other for women, and a dungeon now not used: no court: no water'.

Howard also describes:

'A new building … consisting of six rooms with chimneys. Three of them on the ground-floor are 17 feet by 12, and arched with brick. In one room, the

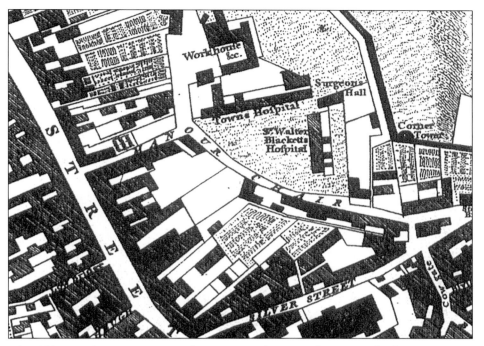

The old house of correction was in this area around Manor Chare, just off Pilgrim Street which is the wide street to the left.

men by a machine, beat hemp and flax. The walls of the court not being secure, the prisoners have no access to it. Their allowance is two pence a day, and firing. The keeper is a sergeant at mace. He has no salary, but the profit of the prisoners work, whom I always found employed. The water is brought near the prison. Clauses against spirituous liquors not hung up.'

According to the Parliamentary Survey of 1818:

The governor receives it* as part of his salary, except the value of labour done by prisoners, who are not sentenced to hard labour, each of whom has received at least one half of his or her earnings.

No food is found for the prisoners; every morning each prisoner is paid 3d with which he is at liberty to purchase such food as he pleases; the prisoners have bedsteads, straw and woollen rugs provided for them, as also coals; there is no allowance of clothing, except in cases of extreme necessity.

The labour is principally teazing of oakum, and there is generally a sufficient quantity of old rope or hemp to keep all the prisoners employed in teazing it, but the profits arising from it are very small: there is a machine for beating flax or hemp, which is seldom put into motion, owing to want of materials. There are no written rules for the house of correction; there are two rooms attached, one for males and another for females, which are under charge of the governor, and he receives such persons into them, as happen to be apprehended by the night watch or patrol, until they can be conveyed before a Magistrate for examination; but in consequence of want of room in the house of correction, he is frequently from necessity obliged to confine in these night prisons persons who are committed for punishment. A new house of correction is in contemplation.

*'it' refers to the value of the labour by prisoners in this institution. The labour was beating hemp to make rope &c., or picking oakum – teasing out old rope to make stuffing for ships fenders, furniture and other purposes. In 1818 the value of the labour amounted only to £6.

The cramped conditions and other problems of the house of correction were described in *A Report of the State of the old Prisons in Newcastle* made by Archibald Reed, Esq., an alderman of Newcastle, on 21st December 1818. Alderman Reed was accompanied on his inspection by the famous architect John Dobson.

The House of Correction contained one receiving room, 17 feet by 12, with two beds, in which thirty-five prisoners had been confined at one time. There was one room, with one bed, for female night prisoners, in which thirty had been confined in one night. There were seven private cells, mostly appropriated to unruly and idle apprentices, or to unexamined prisoners; two rooms for convicted prisoners, and a dark cell for refractory prisoners. Prisoners allowed 3d. per day, besides coals, with straw and four horse-sheets for each bed. No soap and towels allowed. The keeper said, 'The smell in a morning from the receiving room is shocking. I have had eight cases of fever lately. Teasing oakum the only employment. Divine service is never performed. Have had in charge 1500 prisoners this year, and last year 1600.'

The report concludes, 'This prison was extremely clean, and does very great credit to Mr. Scott, the keeper.'

This last inspection of local prisons seems to have prompted the decision to fit out the Keep again for use as a temporary prison.

There were attempts by prisoners to escape from these institutions in the Manors. In 1787 three prisoners, John Brown, William Matthews and Robert Andrew, the latter accused of violently assaulting and beating two young women, managed to escape from the sessions house.

Robert Andrew evaded capture for seventeen months and then was arrested in Newcastle, and the almost inevitable sentence of transportation caught up with him. The report on the Quarter Sessions contains some interesting examples of sentences.

At the General Quarter Sessions of the Peace held here on Wednesday last (April 22nd) seven persons were convicted of larceny; two of those, viz. Robert Andrew, Nailor, and Wm Curry, Labourer, both for stealing poultry, were sentenced to be transported beyond the seas for the term of seven years: The other five were as follows, viz. John Kirk, Labourer, for stealing plough irons, was sentenced to hard labour in the House of Correction till this day at noon and then to be publicly whipped from thence up to and through the Westgate; Margaret Macknairn, otherwise Anderson, for stealing poultry, two months hard labour in the House of Correction and then to be privately whipped, discharged and turned out of town; Geo. Grieve, Smith, a youth, for stealing linen, two months hard labour in the House of Correction, and then to be privately whipped, and discharged; Ann Scott, Spinster, a girl of about 13 years of age, for stealing a table cloth, two months hard labour in the House of Correction; Andrew Smith, Labourer, for stealing a silk handkerchief, one month's hard labour in the House of Correction.

Newcastle Courant Saturday April 25th, 1789

The saga of Robert Andrew does not end there. He and William Curry were transferred to Newgate Gaol to await transportation to New South Wales but on 30th October, they and an accomplice called Roger Carr, also under sentence of transportation, escaped. According to reports, Curry was wearing no breeches at the time of the escape!

This escape from Newgate was a very risky enterprise because escaping from gaol after sentence of transportation carried the death penalty. Andrews and Carr were recaptured. They were sentenced to death at the next Assizes in August 1790 but were reprieved for transportation.

At the same Assizes in 1790 William Sanderson, a boy of 14 years of age, was sentenced to death for burglary. He was convicted of housebreaking at the home Mrs Mary Sowerby in Northumberland Street and stealing 68 guineas cash. Robert Andrew, Roger Carr and William Sanderson went out to Australia in the third fleet of convict ships (see page 98).

The award for the most ingenious escape from the house of correction must go to James Stewart, a petty thief who escaped in 1765. Stewart was a chimney sweep, but his gaoler didn't know that. Put to work beating hemp, Stewart made it into a strong rope, climbed the chimney, lowered himself to the ground with the rope and ran off.

Newgate

The great fortress-like tower of Newgate served Newcastle as the town gaol from around 1400 to 1823 when it was demolished. The earliest account of the inside of Newgate was written by John Howard who made five visits to the gaol between 21st March 1774 and 25th March 1782. However harsh the prison may seem to modern minds, Howard found many things he approved of. The 'firing' mentioned here is coal for the prison fires.

> In this Newgate, which is the gate at the upper end of the town, all the rooms except the condemned room are up stairs, and airy: I always found them remarkably clean, strewed with sand &c. The corporation allow both debtors and felons firing and candles in plenty: and every prisoner has a chaff bed, two blankets, and a coverlet: debtors and felons are thus accommodated in few other prisons in England. They also allow brooms, mops, and all, such necessaries. The sums generously allowed for those articles, amount to £40 12s 8d per annum. This is one of the very few gaols that have what is called in London the rules. Part of two streets near the gaol is in the prison-liberty.
>
> The debtors walk on the battery at the top of the gaol, which is 38 feet by 34 … The debtors' beds are in closets: if on iron bedsteads and in the wards (as in some hospitals) it would be more salutary. No prisoners here have fetters, unless they be riotous. For some years past, prisoners acquitted have been discharged in court; the corporation paid the gaoler's fees if the prisoners were poor. Gaol delivery once a year.
>
> I was concerned to find that the humane gaoler Craster was dead. But his successor Mr. Harle seems equally worthy of the trust.
>
> Dr. Rotheram, a physician in this town, visits the prisoners very assiduously without fee or reward. This is one of the few instances of the kind I have met with.
>
> The act for preserving the health of prisoners was hung up, both on the debtors and felons side. Clauses against spirituous liquors not hung up.
>
> A palisaded wall is erected at a little distance from the felons window, to prevent files &c. being conveyed to them.

The State of the Prisons in England and Wales by John Howard, (4th ed. 1792)

Newgate Prison c.1823.

The coal was not actually funded by the corporation but, at that time, was made available through the generosity of a local gentlemen, Sir Walter Blackett of Heaton, and charged to his estate. He also paid the salary of one of the two chaplains of the gaol.

The gaoler was paid a salary of £50 per annum, (rising to £85 in 1796) £2 gown money (to provide suitable dress for ceremonial occasions), plus some fees, for the prisoners detained on criminal charges. The gaolers were appointed by the Common Council and not by the magistrates, although many members of the council would also have been justices of the peace.

In 1736 there was a scandal at Newgate when Thomas Tate, a turnkey at the gaol, turned to crime. Tate had stolen some pieces of cloth from the shop of a Mr Durance. He gave one to his godchild. Unfortunately, the mother of the child then tried to sell Mr Durance his own cloth. Tate's crime was discovered and he was imprisoned in his own gaol. On 15 July, Tate and another prisoner, Alexander Ogle, escaped from the dungeon, where they had been chained to the wall. Waiting accomplices removed their irons, then the pair returned to the house of Michael

Dawson the gaoler, by forcing two iron bars out of small cellar and picking the lock of the cellar door. The gaoler's house, dating from 1634, stood next to Newgate on the east side. They made their way to Tate's old room, and, undaunted by the sick servant lying asleep in the bed, took the chest containing Tate's clothes back to the cellar. They then dressed themselves in Tate's best clothes, and finally escaped through a window.

Three days later they were arrested near Bellingham, at the home of the father of Tate's sweetheart. They were returned to prison where Tate was chained, but he boasted that he could break out of any irons. Within 15 minutes, and in front of two magistrates and the gaoler, he had done so. A guard was set on both men. In August 1736, they were transported for seven years.

The gaoler's house at Newgate eventually became a famous public house, Bourgognes on Newgate Street. People say that in the cellars there were cells for prisoners and the remains of a tunnel that had once connected the basement of the house to Newgate Gaol. If the basement was being used as an annex to the gaol then having a tunnel to provide a secure connection between the two buildings was a sensible precaution. Bourgoynes public house was demolished to make way for the Eldon Square development late in the 20th century.

Gaolers living on the premises had to beware of the danger to themselves and their families from prisoners but there were also health problems. It is said that there was usually a dreadful stench emanating from 18th century prisons, caused by the lack of hygiene amongst the prisoners and the conditions in which they were detained. John Howard wrote on the subject:

> Air which has been breathed, is made poisonous to a more intense degree, by the effluvia from the sick, and what else in prisons is offensive. My reader will judge of its malignity, when I assure him, that my clothes were in my first journeys so offensive, that in a post-chaise I could not bear the windows drawn up; and was therefore obliged to travel commonly on horseback. The leaves of my memorandum-book were often so tainted, that I could not use it till spreading it an hour or two before the fire: and even my antidote, a vial of vinegar, has, after using it in a few prisons, become intolerably disagreeable. I did not wonder that in those journeys many gaolers made excuses; and did not go with me into the felon's wards.

> *The State of the Prisons*, John Howard 1776

Prisoners in Newgate were constantly testing the security of the gaol. In 1789, three prisoners managed to saw off their irons and remove an iron bar from one of the windows, but they were discovered at the last minute.

The gaoler's house, Bourgognes on Newgate Street, 1964. The date reads 1634.

One would-be escapee was trapped in a most embarrassing fashion. Early in the morning of Sunday March 2nd 1800, John Outerside, Thomas Graham and Richard Lough, escaped from Newgate: by wrenching a bar from the inside of the chimney of their cell. They climbed onto the roof, made the traditional rope from bedding ('bed cloaths'), which they tied to a sun dial on the roof, and climbed down to the field adjoining Gallowgate. Outerside's partner in crime, John Sill, attempted to join the escape, but he was a plump man and got stuck in the chimney. He could not get either up or down until the keepers pulled him back into the cell. Outerside was recaptured near Beamish the same day.

For the medical care of prisoners, local doctors were called in when required. No salary or retainer was paid, the doctors simply submitted bills. The records about the doctor's names and the problems they faced are sparse. The earliest surviving record is a payment of £1 in 1728 to 'Mr George Pig, surgeon, for prisoners in Gaol.' (Quarter Sessions Order Books) John Howard wrote with warm approval of Dr Rotherham of Newcastle upon Tyne 'who visits the prisoners very assiduously without fee or reward.'

More information survives about the chaplains at Newgate Gaol. John Brand recorded a decision by the common council in the 17th century about the appointment of chaplains and their duties.

> 21st June 1676, there was an order of common-council to appoint a minister for reading prayers every Wednesday and Friday, and preaching a sermon to the prisoners confined there, once a month, with an annual salary of £10.
>
> *History of Newcastle upon Tyne* by John Brand, 1789

The chaplains from 1676 to 1765 were all curates at St Andrew's Church, which was next door to Newgate Gaol. In 1765, the common council appointed the curates of St John's and St Andrew's to share the chaplain's duties between them.

The criminal prisoners at Newgate fell into a handful of categories. Firstly those awaiting trial at the Newcastle Assizes – that could be a long wait, anything up to twelve months. By 1819, however, the high judges had begun to hold a winter (or Lent) Assize in March, as well as the traditional late summer sitting in August each year.

Rarely did Newgate hold a prisoner serving a short sentence of imprisonment. There are few examples to be found but here is a report from 1774 which contains evocative images.

At the General Quarter Sessions held here on Wednesday, Alice, wife of David Sinclair, keelman, was convicted of petit larceny and sentenced to be led around the Sandhill and from thence to Sandgate, the first market day with a paper on her forehead and this inscription thereon in large letters 'a notorious thief,' and then to be committed to gaol for two months.

Newcastle Courant Saturday 22nd January 1774

The next category were those prisoners sentenced to death. For murderers only about 48 hours elapsed after sentence before the punishment was carried out, other condemned prisoners usually waited something of the order of two weeks or so after sentence. Next were the prisoners sentenced to transportation, and awaiting a contract ship to carry them to the south of England to join the convict ship fleet. Included amongst those were the prisoners sentenced to death but reprieved by the judges for transportation. They remained in Newgate 12 months waiting confirmation of their pardon and a new sentence of transportation.

There was a very small final category of criminal prisoners being held awaiting escort to other prisons for trial at Assize courts elsewhere, including prisoners who were subject to what were called Habeas Corpus proceedings and, occasionally, deserters. There was less accommodation for criminal prisoners than for debtors in Newgate Gaol. This led to overcrowding, which probably was what lay behind a dangerous situation at the gaol in August 1787.

> **During the absence of the gaoler on Monday, the felons in Newgate became very disorderly, and on Mr Mordue's assistant attempting to put them into separate apartments, one of the villains stabbed him in the side with a knife; but he is happily recovered.**
>
> *Newcastle Courant*, Saturday, 11th August 1787

There were only four rooms in Newgate for male criminal prisoners and one for females. The sexes were separated but otherwise, young and old, tried and untried, the prisoners were simply mixed together. At the time of John Howard's visits, the criminal prisoners had an allowance of two pence per day and by 1818 that allowance had risen to five pence per day.

The practice of confining people to prison for debt spanned more than five centuries. It had its roots in a 14th century statute and was finally brought to an end for all practical purposes by the Abolition of Imprisonment for Debt Act 1880. Debtors were committed to prison at the request of their creditors. It appears the purpose was firstly to ensure the debtors did not escape their responsibilities, and secondly, to bring pressure to bear for family, friends and associates to rally round the debtor and raise the money necessary to obtain his release. But this was not always the case, as some debtors were quite prepared to manipulate the system to persuade their creditors to accept less than the full amount owed to them. Some debtor prisoners spent many years in confinement for small debts and some of those died in prison.

Newgate had six rooms for male debtors and one for females. The two classes mixed freely and men and women shared a kitchen. Their food allowance was twopence per day, rising to fourpence in 1818. The share of available space allocated to the criminal and debtor prisoners clearly indicates that the debtors' side of the gaol was the busiest by far, but less troublesome for the gaoler. Even so the gaoler could find himself in hot water if he failed to keep debtors secure as Gaoler Thomas Harle of Newgate found to his cost in 1783 when Thomas Thompson, a debtor, escaped. His creditor, William Ellison, sued the Sheriff and was awarded damages and costs of £52. Five pounds a quarter was deducted from Harle's salary until the £52 was repaid to the corporation.

The regime for debtors at Newgate was less tough than for criminals. They were not put in irons and, if they had some personal resources or support from outside, their day-to-day life could be made more comfortable. They were permitted to walk on the 'lead flats' roof of Newgate – it was covered with lead to make it water-tight. In 1814, Edward Wiggan, a debtor from Bedlington, was walking with the other prisoners on the roof when he leapt off the fifty foot high building and into a nearby dunghill. He sank up to his knees in dung, so broke no bones during the fall, but was so shaken by the experience, that he could not continue his escape plan. At first, it was thought he would die, but he did eventually recover.

Some trusted debtors were allowed to walk inside the town walls in Newgate Street between the groined arch gate-way of Newgate and a stream which ran across Newgate Street from Darn Crook (now St Andrew's Street). That point was called 'Execution Dock' and was about 40 yards or so from Newgate. 'Dock' is an old English word for a stream, so it was the 'Execution Stream', but why it was so called is lost in antiquity.

Walking was more than simply gentle exercise for George Wilson, a debtor, who in 1813 made a bet that he could walk 50 miles within 12 hours inside the prison walls. He walked round and round a yard measuring 33 feet by 25 feet 6ins. He finished his challenge just four minutes and forty three seconds within the stipulated time. He was, presumably, very dizzy, but £3 is richer, as he had won his bet. He went on to build something of a career from his walking and is reported to have performed various feats of pedestrianism in Newcastle, London and other places.

The Newcastle historian, John Baillie, included a brief account of Newgate in his work, but he made no mention of his own connection with the place. John Baillie was a Presbyterian minister. In 1767 he was settled into a position as minister to a large Presbyterian congregation at the Sallyport Meeting House which stood between Sallyport Tower and the Keelmen's Hospital. John Baillie was a man of 'convivial habits'; drinking led to mismanagement of his affairs and that brought him to Newgate Gaol as a debtor prisoner about 1781. Richard Welford continues the story.

> In those days the authorities allowed ministers who were in gaol for debt to go out and preach on the Sabbath, of course in charge of an officer. This officer was bound to see the minister safely lodged in gaol when the duties of the day were over. Mr Baillie persuaded the officer one Sabbath to give him his liberty, promising to return to the gaol in the evening. He did not keep his word, but fled to Scotland.
>
> *Men of Mark Twixt Tyne and Tweed* by Richard Welford, 1894

However, some way was found to clear the debts of John Baillie and he came back to Tyneside. Heavy drinking spoiled a promising talent and career; he was said to have been an eloquent preacher and a writer of fine quality, but his life was dogged by debt and he died in 1806 aged 66 years.

When Joseph John Gurney and his sister Elizabeth Fry visited Newgate Gaol on 25th August 1818 they commented that the magistrates 'have it seriously in contemplation to erect a new jail.' In fact Newgate lasted just five more years. Gurney and Fry found much to criticise in Newgate:

> The Jail at Newcastle, like the Old Jail at Durham is a tower built over a gateway, and like that prison is extremely ill adapted to its purpose. On the left side of the gateway as you enter the town from the north there are three small rooms for felons measuring respectively about fourteen feet square. These rooms have severally a window looking into the street, through which the prisoners have an easy opportunity of communicating with the people who are passing below. On the ground floor there is a cold and miserable

Dungeon, now happily disused. There is also on this side of the prison a court-yard measuring sixty feet by eighteen; but as the walls which surround this yard are considerably insecure, the prisoners are never allowed to walk in it except in the presence of the jailer. There were at this time four men felons in the prison, two together in a room. Some of these prisoners appeared to have derived much advantage from the kind care and instruction of a benevolent lady, who had frequently visited them. One of them, who was going off for the hulks on the following day, earnestly begged for a bible to take with him. The felons in this prison are allowed five-pence per day. They are heavily ironed, and may be fastened, at the jailer's pleasure, to an iron ring fixed in the floor of their cells.

The manner in which they are confined is extremely objectionable. Having no access to the yard or any sleeping cells, they pass both day and night in their small day-room, without change or intermission…

On the opposite side of the prison, called the Debtors' side, and on the right of the gateway as you enter the town, there are two more small rooms used occasionally for felons. In one of those we observed a wretched woman, committed on the charge of murdering her child, but apparently insane, in solitary confinement, and looking out of her window on the street below. The accommodation for debtors consists of one large day-room and six small lodging rooms without fire places, the doors of the latter opening into the former; also a small court-yard, of which the debtors make but little use, as they prefer taking their exercise on the leads at the top of the prison. There is no effectual separation between the men and women debtors. There was at this time one of the latter descriptions in the jail. We found her in one of the small lodging rooms already mentioned, to which she could have no access except through the men's day-room. We have seldom observed a female in prison so fearfully exposed to danger. As the faults of this prison may be traced chiefly to the inadequacy of the building, it gives me much pleasure to state, that the magistrates of Newcastle – who are justly celebrated for the excellence of their police establishment – have it serious in contemplation to erect a new gaol.

Notes made on a visit to some of The Prisons in Scotland and the North of England, in company with Elizabeth Fry by Joseph John Gurney, Edinburgh, 1819

There had been rumblings of dissatisfaction about Newgate for years but the final push to replace the gaol had its roots in Alderman Reed's inspection of 1818. The gaol was presented at the Lent Assizes in 1820 as being 'insufficient and out of repair.' Newgate was closed and demolished in 1823. The *Newcastle Courant* celebrated the removal of 'an unsightly nuisance from one of the principal streets', and commented that recycling of the old stones would save the inhabitants of Newcastle considerable expense.

The authorities required interim arrangements for criminal and debtor prisoners until the new prison in Carliol Square was put up and ready to receive prisoners. The Keep now belonged to Newcastle and it was decided to use the old basement prison as a temporary gaol for criminal prisoners of the town.

Castlegarth today is an open area with easy access to the fine public buildings, the Moot Hall and the former County Hall, the Keep, Black Gate and the ramparts at the top of the ancient Castle Stairs. There are wonderful views of the Tyne and the bridges across the river. But in the 18th century it was a different story. This piece of county land inside Newcastle was then crowded with houses and other

buildings. There were shops and dwellings built close up to the arch of Black Gate and to the Keep and the old Moot Hall. The county authorities required accommodation for prisoners at Castlegarth for about seven days each year during the sitting of the Northumberland Assize Court in the old Moot Hall and also for two or three days for a sitting of the General Quarter Sessions for Northumberland. The prisoners were put into the basement dungeon of the Keep. The practice continued into the 19th century until the first sitting of the Northumberland Assizes in the new Moot Hall in August 1812. The new court building included a secure cell complex in the basement.

The Black Gate and Castlegarth, with its winding alleys, photographed in the late 19th century.

Two very old cellars or underground chambers used for prisoners, strictly called oubliettes, have survived in Castlegarth. Entering Black Gate from St Nicholas Street today and passing through the arch, the old cobbled road turns to the right. Just a few yards along from the arch and on the right is exposed a chamber of great stone blocks below the ground level, that is the Heron Pit dating from 1347, so-called after William Heron, Sheriff of Northumberland 1247-1257. Entry to the Heron Pit was originally gained by means of a trap door from the gaoler's house above. This prison-cellar, which had no light or sanitation facilities, replaced an earlier Heron Pit at or near the same site and dating back to the middle of the 13th century. On the left is another former prison cellar called the Great Pit also dating from 1347.

The Newcastle authorities came to an agreement with the Northumberland county magistrates to lease the cell complex in the basement of the new Moot Hall in Castlegarth to house the Newcastle criminal prisoners for the four or five years it took to build the Carliol Square Gaol. Strictly speaking, its tale falls outside of the period covered in this book, but the story is an important and interesting one.

Carliol Square Gaol

The man chosen to design the new gaol was the famous local architect, John Dobson. In 1823 Dobson was also working on a new prison for Northumberland at Morpeth and was establishing a reputation for the design of prisons.

A site in Carliol Croft, in front of the new Clergy Jubilee School, was finally selected and acquired at a cost of £2,000. It was an open area inside the town walls which was to become known as Carliol Square. It was not a popular choice, because of the distance from the courts at Sandhill. Historian, Eneas Mackenzie commented that moving prisoners on foot through the streets, would expose petty offenders, women and young people to the attentions of an unsympathetic public. However within ten years that particular problem was solved as in 1837 a police station and magistrates court, designed by John Dobson, were opened in Manors quite close to the prison.

The foundation stone for the gaol was laid by the mayor, Robert Bell, on 4th June 1823 and it took nearly five years to complete the building. The first prisoner arrived a month earlier than expected and was a man of considerable notoriety. On 1st February 1829 York Minster was deliberately set on fire and enormous damage was caused to this ancient and revered place of worship. The person responsible was Jonathan Martin (1782-1838) of Hexham the brother of the famous artist John Martin. He spent two hours in Carliol Square Gaol on Sunday 8 February on his way from Hexham to York to stand trial.

At the end of February the local newspapers were carrying reports about the new gaol in Carliol Square being ready to receive prisoners and this is typical example:

> **The Newcastle Gaol and House of Correction have now been completed and the prisoners will be transferred from the old castle in the course of the present week. We believe for convenience and for security these prisons will not yield to any in the kingdom. There is not a particle of wood in the whole fabric, it is formed entirely of stone and iron. The expense of the buildings has been near the estimates, namely about thirty-three thousand pounds.**
>
> *The Tyne Mercury* Tuesday 26th February 1828

There are various local historical sources describing this 'New Prison' including this succinct description from a mid-19th century guide to the town:

> On the west side of Carliol Square is the entrance to the Gaol and House of Correction by a porter's lodge, with two floors of rooms above. The site of these prisons contain an area of about two acres of ground, enclosed by a substantial stone wall, 25 feet high … The design by Mr John Dobson, architect, on the radiated principle of single buildings, with airing yards adjoining. In the centre stands the governor's house, with apartments for the turnkey and matron; over which, in the semicircular part, is the chapel, from which a veranda and metal bridges conduct to the upper stories of the radiated buildings. The debtors' prison is on the north side, and the House of Correction is on the south side of the governor's house. On the east are three other buildings, with airing yards, enclosed by a stone wall 14 feet high, and metal railings at the end fronting the governor's house. An order from a magistrate is required previous to viewing the interior of these prisons.
>
> *A Guide to Newcastle upon Tyne*, James Corbridge, 1851

Dobson's design laid out the cell blocks in a radial system so that the windows of one block faced out on to the blank wall of the next to prevent communication. The principles aimed at in this new institution were safe custody, punishment and reformation. Many compliments were paid to John Dobson and the authorities believed that they had done everything they could to provide Newcastle with a fine secure prison to meet all the demands of the 19th century. However, within just ten years prison standards had changed so much that the building was no longer acceptable. The frustration was intense and the situation was constantly worsening. The gathering impact of professional police forces was causing the prison popula-

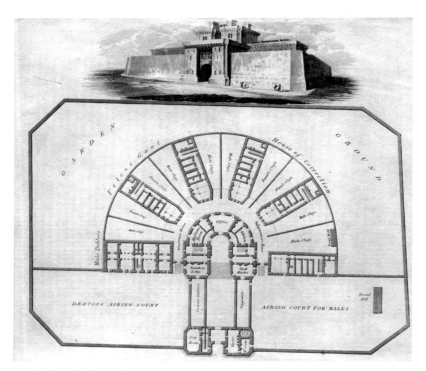

The grim facade of John Dobson's Carliol Square gaol from the architect's plan. The original design showed six blocks but only five were actually built.

tions to grow and not far ahead lay the end of transportation and the need for a strategy to deal with long term prisoners. Eventually drastic reforms and alterations had to be made by John Dobson. The gaol passed into the control of the Prison Commissioners in 1877. Northumberland prisoners were transferred to Carliol Square from Morpeth when the gaol there was closed by the commissioners on 20th October 1881. The prison at Newcastle was also ear-marked for closure for many years before it actually came about. The commissioners did not see it as suitable for development given the location, restricted site and the age of the buildings and it was closed on 31st March 1925.

There were a number of escapes from the Carliol Square Gaol but for sheer nerve, skill and ingenuity Robert Boyd's escape in 1858 would be hard to beat. Here is Thomas Fordyce's account of it transcribed from local newspapers.

6TH AUGUST 1858. A notorious fellow, named Robert Boyd, 22 years of age, who had been sentenced to six years' penal servitude by Mr. Baron Martin for being concerned in a garrotte robbery, effected his escape from Newcastle

Gaol, in a most daring and clever manner. He had been lodged in a cell in one of the wings facing the governor's private residence, and, on the morning on which he made his escape, or on the night proceeding, he had succeeded in forcing from its place, by means of a cold chisel, a large metal pipe near the roof of his prison, thus making an aperture nine inches in breadth and fourteen inches in length through which he squeezed himself and got on to the roof. Having procured a number of rugs and knotted them together, so as to form a stout rope, he passed from the top of the building to a gallery, from thence to another gallery immediately opposite to the governor's sleeping room, then to a gallery above, and having crossed a foot-bridge he then dropped to the ground. He then proceeded to the stone breaking yard, obtained a plank and two bags of teazed hair, with which to assist himself in escaping, and re-ascending the wall, by means of a plank, gained the spot he had just left. The wall which he had ascended, is furnished with a cheveux de frize,* upon this he placed the bags of hair to prevent it from revolving, and having placed the plank upon it, he clambered up the wall and descended on the other side in Carliol-square. All these operations were performed at the most imminent hazard and risk of detection but so cleverly were they executed that the escape was not discovered until three o'clock, when a policeman saw the rugs suspended from the gaol wall. Every effort was made for the discovery of the escaped prisoner, but all exertions were fruitless until three weeks afterwards, when Boyd was apprehended by two county police officers, after a desperate resistance, at the house of a relative in the neighbourhood of St Anthony's.

Historical Register of Remarkable Events, Thomas Fordyce, 1876

(*cheveux de frize – a revolving spiked security device for preventing persons climbing over walls.)

The buildings and land were sold to Newcastle Council but before the prison could be demolished there was a problem to be dealt with. After 1829 the bodies of executed prisoners were buried within the precincts of the prison and there were 15 graves within the prison. Authority was given by the Secretary of State for the graves to be opened in the autumn of 1925, the remains taken up and reburied in All Saints Cemetery, Jesmond Road. All the graves were opened up but the remains of only eleven bodies were found. There was one empty coffin. The authorities concluded that the bodies not recovered had been passed to the surgeons many years earlier for medical research. Another skeleton was found during the digging of foundations for new buildings on the site.

5 Punishments of the Past

> '*Called the new fashioned cloak and so to make them march to the view of all beholders; and this was their punishment for drunkards and the like.*'
>
> *England's Grievance Discovered*, Ralph Gardner 1655

The cruel and unusual punishments that were employed before, and in some cases during, the 18th century are mercifully no longer in the statute book. They were all intended to expose offenders to public humiliation, discomfort and often a great deal of pain. By the 18th century many had fallen out of use.

The Drunkard's Cloak or the Barrel of Shame

The Drunkard's Cloak was more famously known as the 'Newcastle Cloak', because there is no record of it being used anywhere else in the United Kingdom. Drunken offenders were paraded around the streets with a barrel over their head and arms. There is a record of its use in Newcastle as late as 1672 but there is no surviving record of the cloak being used in the 18th century on Tyneside though it was in use outside Great Britain at the time.

In the 1650s Ralph Gardner, a landowner of Chirton near Tynemouth, was in dispute with the authorities at Newcastle about the monopoly of the coal trade on the Tyne. In 1655 he published a collection of documents supporting his claims under the title *England's Grievance Discovered in Relation to the Coal-Trade*.

One of Gardner's grievances concerned the conduct of the magistrates at Newcastle, and he included amongst the papers a deposition from John Willis, a ship's master of Ipswich, describing the use of the Drunkard's Cloak:

> He, this deponent, further affirms, that he hath seen men drove up and down the streets with a great tub or barrel opened at the sides with hole in one end, to put through their heads, and so to cover their shoulders and bodies, down to the small of their legs, and then close the same, called the new fashioned

The Drunkard's Cloak, right, and the Branks, illustrated by Ralph Gardner.

cloak, and so make them march to the view of all beholders; and this was their punishment for drunkards or the like.

There is no record of a similar punishment being used anywhere in the United Kingdom. There is just one more local record about this punishment in the Chamberlain's Account Books. In October 1672 the authorities at Newcastle paid the Whipper and Hougher his quarter-year salary and a fee for putting an offender into the 'kittewate.' The word 'kittewate' does not appear in the Oxford English Dictionary but the definitions for the two elements of it are telling. A 'kitte' was 'a small barrel', 'wate' meant 'the weight of shame or blame', therefore, the whole word 'kittewate' means the 'the barrel of shame'.

It seems probable that the concept of the Newcastle Cloak for dealing with offenders came to Newcastle by way of the extensive shipping trade with the countries of mainland Europe. There are records of the use of similar devices in The Hague, Copenhagen, and even on a convict ship bound for New South Wales.

The Branks

The Branks was an unpleasant and potentially damaging device for punishing women accused of being malicious gossips. Ralph Gardner notes:

He (John Willis) was in Newcastle six months ago and there saw one Ann Bidlestone drove through the streets by an officer of the same corporation hold-

The Newcastle branks.

ing a rope in his hands, the other end fastened to an engine called the branks, which is like a crown; it being of iron which was musled (sic), over the head and face, with a great gap or tongue of iron forced into her mouth, which forced the blood out; and that is the punishment which magistrates do inflict on upon chiding and scoulding women; and that he hath seen the like done to others.

The use of the branks is well documented throughout the United Kingdom including Newcastle and a well preserved example is held in Tyne and Wear Museums. It was like the skeleton of a helmet, made of strips of iron running back to front and side to side over the head and joining a hoop passing around the head, level with the mouth. The strips were hinged at the top and sides and at the front there was a triangular hole for the nose. The purpose of the branks was to keep the tongue still with a wedge of iron that protruded into the mouth from the nose hole. As the hinged strips were closed around the head the wedge was held in place.

In the case of the Newcastle Branks the wedge of iron is smooth but in many other examples of the branks the wedge or tongue was serrated like a file or was arrow shaped with sharp points. Movement or resistance against the constraint of the branks could and did lead to damage to the tongue and flesh of the mouth. In Newcastle the offender was led around the town by one of the town sergeants holding a rope attached to the branks. It was common for the offender to have a paper notice attached to their clothing describing the nature of their offence.

The Chamberlain's Account Books at Newcastle upon Tyne for March 1645 contain payments for making branks: 'pd Rob: Gillis ffor making one pare of branks as p bill 13s 4d.' Six months later Robert Gillis was paid 26s 8d for making two more pairs of branks, so by the middle of the 17th century Newcastle had three sets. Perhaps the surviving set of branks at Newcastle was made by Gillis, it is certainly very old but there are no makers' marks on it to confirm the age.

No records survive to show when the branks was last used in Newcastle but there is a note of its use at Morpeth in the 18th century:

3rd December 1741 Elizabeth wife of George Holborn was punished with the branks for two hours at the market cross Morpeth by order of Mr Thomas Gait and Mr George Nicholls then bailiffs for scandalous and opprobrious language to several persons in the town as well as to the bailiffs.

It is said that the last use of the branks in the United Kingdom took place in Lancashire in 1856. This unpleasant device seems to have only been used between the 16th century and the early 19th century.

The Ducking Stool

Another way of dealing with the scold and malicious gossip was the Ducking Stool. It was also used to punish other community offences such as tradesmen selling with short measure or bad quality bread. This punishment is said to have its roots in a Celtic practice of drowning offenders in a cage in rivers and other bodies of water. It is mentioned in the Domesday Book at Chester and it begins to come to notice in Northumberland in the 13th century when various barons, for example at Corbridge, Whalton, Newburn, Rothbury and Elsdon, claimed at the Northumberland Assizes in 1293 and 1294 a baronial right to use the ducking stool or tumbrel and other things such as a gallows.

The ducking stool was essentially a seat to which an offender was strapped and by some means plunged into a pond or river, thoroughly humiliating and soaking them but not drowning them. It may have been suspended by a block and tackle from a suitable point above water or fixed to a beam across a post and operated see-saw fashion. This sort of device was easily fitted to a bridge to duck offenders in a river.

The tumbrel was a ducking stool fitted to the end of a beam and carried on a set of wheels for parading offenders such as scolds and dishonest tradesmen before the community, perhaps with a notice proclaiming their offence. The tumbrel

could be pushed into water with the beam upended to sink the offender. A refinement was to fit the chair with a toilet seat. It was then known as a cuck stool and added further to the humiliation of the victim.

In 1562 there were proceedings in the Durham ecclesiastical court brought by Janet Clerk for defamation against Agnes Aydon, a member of the Northumbrian Brandling family and another woman. Aydon was alleged to have said to Clerk:

> Go thy way, like nowt as thou art, and cut a purse, as thou has done before time, and thou may be ducked in the Tyne as thou has been.
>
> *History of Newcastle and Gateshead*, Richard Welford, 1885

The quote has a Shakespearean ring to it and is evidence that the River Tyne was used for ducking offenders, presumably by block and tackle from the medieval bridge across the Tyne or from the quay. The expression 'cut a purse' refers to the old practice of carrying a bag called a purse for money and other things suspended from a belt. Deft thieves would slit the purse with a very sharp knife, catch the valuables and make off with the goods Such offenders were known as cut purses.

Peine Fort et Dure

Conviction of felony led to forfeiture to the crown of the offender's land, money and goods. It was possible to escape the forfeiture by pleading neither Guilty nor Not Guilty to the indictment – staying silent in other words – and in this way the offender's family would not be left destitute.

The trial could not proceed without a plea. To force the prisoner to offer a plea he was laid naked, except for a loincloth, on the ground, usually in prison. Iron weights, sufficient to crush him, were laid on his body and were increased daily. The prisoner was given three drinks of stagnant water one day and three morsels of stale bread the following day but not both on the same day. This continued until the prisoner died or offered a plea. There are examples in England back to the 13th century. Eventually, in 1827, the law was changed and a plea of Not Guilty was entered for prisoners refusing to plead or not making their intention clear. That remains the case today.

Only three examples of pressing have come to light in the North East. Thomas Bowland was pressed to death, for an unknown offence, on 7th August 1578 on Palace Green, Durham. Anthony Arrowsmith was arraigned for murder on 26th August 1597, stood mute at his trial and was pressed to death in the market place. At Newcastle in 1676 either Thomas Chaitor or Thomas Scott refused to plead to sheep stealing until the press was made ready and then quickly changed his mind.

Whipping

Whipping, in public and private, was widespread in England. Whipping of disobedient servants was widely practised. Town and parish officials, Sergeants, Beadles and Marshals would either carry out the whipping or cause it to be done under their supervision. Public whipping posts were common throughout the country and some still survive to this day. The public pillory often doubled as a whipping post.

Whipping was extensively used in Tudor times for such problems as the control of beggars and vagrants, idle people refusing to work, runaway servants and prostitutes. It is said that there were 60 whipping posts, stocks and cages in London in 1630. The Commonwealth Act of 1650 set death as a punishment for adultery (for women that is) and whipping as a punishment for fornication and male adultery.

Men, women, and children were whipped without discrimination and Newcastle records make many references to punishment by whipping. In 1561 Gawan Aydon, the town sergeant, was paid 16 pence for 'squrgying' a boy about the town. Such entries continue until 100 years later when the Whipper and Hougher of Swine appears in the account books.

In the early days the Whipper and Hougher was paid one shilling per whipping over and above his quarterly salary. Sentences at the Quarter Sessions would often be coupled with a short sentence of confinement in the House of Correction, an establishment that was part workhouse, part prison and part place of hard labour for offenders. The favoured way of whipping offenders at Newcastle was not the whipping post but a moving procession through the streets ensuring maximum discomfort and humiliation for the offender. The Recorder and Magistrates would specify the date and time, starting point, route through the streets and the finishing point for the whipping. The offender, man or woman, was stripped to the waist, then with hands tied to the back of a cart was led along the ordered route being whipped meanwhile by the Whipper and Hougher.

Usually the crime is shown in the court records as petit larceny – stealing of goods below the value of one shilling, thereby avoiding the death penalty. The distance for the whipping procession varied considerably. Here are two examples of whipping along a short distance:

Newcastle Quarter Sessions Order Book July 1743-April 1777

Easter Sessions 1776 (17th April)

William Coulson, Butcher for stealing a side of veal the property of John Thompson, ordered that he be taken from hence to the House of Correction and kept at hard labour until Saturday next at twelve o'clock then publickly

Thomas Bewick's depiction of whipping, from Aesop's Fables.

whipt from the foot of the Flesh Market to Newgate, then discharged.

Newcastle Quarter Sessions Order Book July 1743 – April 1777

Midsummer Sessions 1776.

Ann Pringle wife of William Pringle convicted of petit larceny (stealing the goods of Richard Stephens and Francis Lambert) ordered that she be taken from hence to the House of Correction in this town and then be kept at hard labour until Saturday next at twelve of the clock and that she be then brought from thence and whipt from the Head of the Side to the North end of the Bridge in this town and then discharged.

But there are also examples of prisoners literally whipped from one end of the town to the other, starting at Newgate Prison adjoining St Andrew's Church, along Newgate Street, down the Bigg Market past St Nicholas Church and down the Side around Sandhill up to the Blue Stone in the centre of the old Tyne Bridge:

Newcastle Quarter Sessions Order Book 1718-1719

1718 Ann Camble a lewd vagrant haveing been guilty of severall Crimes. It is ordered that on Saturday next betwixt the hours of twelve and one she be whipped from the Newgate to the Blew Stone on the Bridge.

Newcastle Quarter Sessions Order Book July 1743-April 1777

Easter Sessions 1744

Mary Train, spinster, stealing from Henry Milburn Butcher, to be publickly whipt from the Newgate to the Blue Stone on the Bridge for the said offence.

We can only speculate whether the authorities expected the Whipper and Hougher to carry out these sentences all on one day, a long part of the route for whipping Turnbull and Heslop lay uphill:

Newcastle Quarter Sessions Order Book July 1743-April 1777

Midsummer Sessions 1744

Isabell Turnbull spinster stealing two hammers from Francis Gilmore, to be publickly whipt from the Blue Stone on the Bridge to Newgate;
Mary Johnson getting clothing by false pretences, to be publickly whipt from Newgate to the Blue Stone on the Bridge;
Sarah Heslop stealing linen shirt to be publickly whipt from Blue Stone on the Bridge to Newgate.

The whipping of women in public ended in 1817 and was abolished altogether in 1820.

In the 19th century whipping was still seen as an appropriate punishment for many offences, although the practice of public whipping ceased. Whippings and birching in prison continued on to the middle of the 20th century and was finally brought to an end by the Criminal Justice Act of 1948.

One final example on the topic of whipping offenders:

> **Monday (26th June) a man who had made a practice of drinking in ale houses, without paying, was ordered out of town by the magistrates. but, having been detected in the same practice the day following, he was on Wednesday, tied to a cart, and severly whipped from the Sandhill to Westgate, where he was discharged.**
>
> *Newcastle Chronicle* Saturday 1st July 1786

The Pillory or the Norway Neck-cloth

The pillory and the stocks were a common sight in Newcastle in the 18th century; there were pillories in Newgate Street, the Flesh Market and Sandhill.

At first glance the stocks and pillory seem much the same thing, both were devices for confining offenders in public exposing them to humiliation and abuse from the community and to be pelted with anything unpleasant and dangerous the people could lay their hands on. However, the pillory was the more dangerous device of the two. With the stocks the offender was sitting down with only his legs confined and his hands were free to protect his head and body.

In the case of the pillory the offender was standing with his head locked through boards and his hands locked or strapped in the same way. There was much less chance to avoid things thrown at him and he was exposed to the likelihood of strangulation if he fainted or became exhausted. It is hardly surprising, therefore, that there are records of several deaths in the pillory, though there were none in the North East that have come to notice.

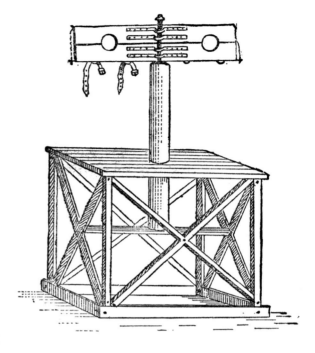

There was a near fatality at Newcastle on 11th April 1758, when Susannah Fleming was put into the pillory at the White Cross Newgate Street for fortune telling, as reported in the Tyneside newspapers:

On Tuesday (i.e. 11th April) Susannah Fleming stood in the Pillory, at the White Cross, Newcastle, an hour pursuant to her Sentence for the first Time (being to stand once in a Quarter for a year), for Fortune-telling; who, tho' not molested by the Populace, was nearly strangled before the Time was expired, occasioned either by fainting and shrinking down, or some say by tying too much about her Neck, and being thereby straitned in the Hole. It is believed she would not have got down alive, had it not been for the Activity of a Sailor, who out of Charity, run up the Ladder and brought her down on his back.

Newcastle Journal Saturday 15th April 1758

She was due to stand for an hour in the pillory once a quarter for a year and it is not recorded whether the remainder of the sentence was carried out.

It is said that use of the stocks and pillory in Britain dates back to Anglo Saxon times. In Newcastle the pillory was used to punish a variety of offences from fraud to petty theft.

> Last Tuesday John Hall alias Tricky Hall, stood in the Pillory, between the hours of Twelve and Two, in the Flesh Market in this Town, for erazing a Receipt upon a Bond, when he was severely pelted by the Populace.
>
> *Newcastle Courant* 21st August 1736

In 1766 the pillory at Sandhill Newcastle upon Tyne was temporarily occupied by an interesting woman called Jean Grey. Her home was in High Bridge at Newcastle and she was famous for making mutton pies. Jean Grey had a lover named Thomas Jameson. In August 1766 Jameson was prosecuted at the Newcastle Assizes on a charge of forging a £5 bank note and Jean Grey was charged with uttering (passing into circulation) the note.

At the trial of Thomas Jameson, Jean Grey gave false evidence on his behalf and Jameson was acquitted. The judge ordered an extra indictment, for perjury, against Grey and her own trial was all over in an hour or so. She was convicted of uttering the forged note and perjury. She was sentenced to stand for one hour in the pillory before being transported to Virginia for seven years. The *Newcastle Advertizer* reported upwards of 6,000 spectators witnessed Grey stand in the pillory on Sandhill between 11.30am and 12.30pm and the crowd:

> behaved with great decency and humanity. At the time of her standing in the pillory pickpockets were very dextrous, several losing their handkerchiefs and one in particular in the crowd his watch.

On Friday 15th August 1766, Jean Grey, with other convicts from Northumberland, Durham and Newcastle and 21 indentured servants were put on board the *Mary* at Shields for transportation to America and the ship sailed the following Sunday. It was common for convicts to be carried south in this way to be gathered together on the Thames or the South coast for final transport across the Atlantic. The *Advertizer* report added this: 'It is said she sailed with undaunted spirits having provided a great many millinery articles intending to set up in that business when she arrives at her intended port.'

Jean Grey returned to Newcastle upon Tyne after serving her sentence and her mutton pies were in greater demand than before! She must have led a very interesting life and it is a pity no one wrote an account of it.

In the 18th century the pillory was sometimes referred to as the 'Norway Neckcloth' because it was usually made from Norway Fir. Use of the pillory was abolished in 1837.

The Stocks

The stocks has a similar but literally more parochial history. There are references in the early statutes to the stocks as early as 1227 and there were Stocks Acts of 1350, 1376 and in the act of 1405 it was stated that the absence of a pair of stocks downgraded a village to a mere hamlet! There were stocks to be found in most of the parishes of the North East. Conduct leading to a spell in the stocks included refusal to work, drunkenness, unruly behaviour, gambling, scolding and failing to abstain from flesh meats in Lent. Disobedient servants were also at risk.

It was common to see stocks in churchyards, St Nicholas Parish Church (now the cathedral) at Newcastle had stocks. They were used in 1826 for a drunken joiner who was put in the stocks for two hours after he had disturbed the congregation by shouting 'Bell for ever.' The parliamentary elections had recently ended with Matthew Bell being elected.

The Chamberlains' Account Books have many entries on the subject of stocks. One in particular of October 1596 records payments for making two new pairs of stocks and repairing a third so there were at least three pairs in the town that year. These records reveal stocks at various locations: 1508 at Sandhill; 1597, October at the White Cross Newgate Street; 1836, August at Sandhill. In addition to the stocks inside the town walls there were also pairs of stocks on county land just outside the walls. In 1691 the people living in Westgate were threatened with a penalty of forty shillings if they failed to put up a new set of stocks.

6 Cargoes of Convicts

> This week three felons confined in Newgate and five or six from Morpeth Jail for knaveries etc. were shipped on board the Marlborough, John Berry, Commander now lying at Shields ready to sail for Nova Scotia.
>
> *Newcastle Courant* 21st April 1753

Transportation, the practice of sending convicted criminals overseas and putting them to work, started in Great Britain at the beginning of the 17th century. It not only rid the country of undesirables, it also provided labour for the nation's rapidly spreading colonial territories. By the middle of the 17th century, hundreds of convicts were being shipped across the Atlantic to Virginia, Maryland, Massachusetts, New England and other colonies such as Jamaica, Barbados and the Leeward Islands to work on the plantations.

The county authorities paid a fee to private contractors to transport the convicts across the seas. On arrival at the colony the convicts were sold to plantation owners and farmers in need of workers. That is how the agents made their profits, they simply saw the convicts as cargo outward bound from Great Britain. Often enough the cargo inward bound was tobacco. The convicts served as slave labour for the period of their sentence, usually seven years, 14 years, or life. In some ways it sounds an ideal solution to providing labour to develop the new colonies. But the reality, of course, was quite different. These convicts were not skilled, well motivated, industrious workers. The governors of the colonies quickly discovered that the convicts were unfit physically and mentally for the work, most of them were idle, shiftless, dishonest men and women, some diseased, who brought nothing but trouble. Eventually some governors refused to take any more convicts, in particular females. Given the great numbers, there was no way the authorities could effectively monitor the treatment or work conditions of the convicts.

The authorities in Great Britain dismissed these objections and, in 1717-18, passed the Transportation Act which increased the range of convicts liable for transportation. There was also a provision for merchants to contract with persons aged over 15 years but under 21 years to enter into voluntary agreement to be transported to America to obtain employment. It was a very early form of government training scheme whereby idle young people were given the chance of work abroad to save them from a possible future life of crime. The effect of this new act was seen

immediately at the Northumberland Assizes on 3rd August 1719, when John, alias George, Scott was convicted of felony. Under the new act he faced transportation to Virginia or Maryland for seven years.

The Transportation Act had a dramatic effect on the rate of transportation from the local courts. In the 45 years from 1673 to 1718 there were 33 convicts transported from the Northumberland and Newcastle courts combined, that is to say less than one per year. Most of these convicts were transported to Barbados. From 1718 to 1775, a period of 57 years, there were 280 convicts transported from the two courts, which is close to five per year.

There were only a handful of contractors authorised to transport convicts during the 18th century; Jonathan Forward 1718-1742, Andrew Reid 1742-1763 and John Stewart and Duncan Campbell 1763-1776 and Duncan Campbell (alone) 1776.

The system adopted by the Newcastle and Northumberland justices was to put the convicts on a ship in the Tyne for movement to the south, usually to the Thames, to join up with the convict ship that was to cross the ocean. The justices at quarter sessions usually appointed two or three of their number to act on their behalf and enter into contracts with the ship's masters and crown agents.

The charge for transporting each convict varied during the century from £5 to £6 10s od. Such movements of the convicts were often reported in the local newspapers:

Last Friday Durham Hills, formerly schoolmaster in Sandgate, with Edward Matthews, was put on board the Owners Goodwill, Captain Moorland in order to be transported to South Carolina for seven years, agreeable to their sentences at last Christmas Sessions for this town.

Newcastle Gazette Wednesday 15th April 1752

If the ship's captain failed to keep the convicts secure, embarrassing proceedings followed as Captain Giles discovered in 1729, when two convicts escaped and he then had to agree to carry three others without charge.

Northumberland Quarter Sessions Order Book 1727 – 1742

Christmas Quarter Sessions 14th January 1729/30

Captain John Hodgshon who by bond with Captain Giles contracted for and suffered two ffellons under transportation to escape. Captain Giles now in Court undertaking to contract for & transport three other ffellons gratis & what number were there now is at five pounds each these. Hodgshons bond on his so doing to be delivered up.

Captain Giles continued in the transportation business none the worse for losing two prisoners.

Moving convicts south by ship was by the far the simplest method and probably the most secure if the numbers were high. But frequently it fell to the county or town gaoler to move the convicts by land, occasionally over a long distance, which added to the expense and security risk. The journey was not always to the south.

The same day (Tuesday 15th August 1758) three felons for Transportation were brought here from Morpeth Gaol, and were, with 16 others from Newgate sent off to Hull, in order to be shipped for the Plantations.

Newcastle Courant Saturday 19th August 1758

If a convict had financial resources, life could be made more comfortable in many ways; on the sea journey special cabin and food arrangements could be made and the convict could avoid being sold into slavery. Take, for example, the case of Jean Grey (see page 87) of Newcastle who took with her into banishment stores of millinery articles intending to set up in that business during her sentence.

Returning from America was simple enough providing the convicts could escape from the plantations and raise money for the passage. Many a ship's captain would turn a blind eye to the obvious and give them a berth or even take the escapee on as crew if they

The American destination of many convicts sentenced to transportation, from Thomas Kitchin's 1771 map

were short-handed. Returning to Great Britain unlawfully after transportation, however, carried the ultimate penalty if caught – death. The infamous border thief, William Brown, known as 'Sir' William Brown, discovered that to his cost.

> Monday 8th August 1743. William Brown, a bold and desperate man, who was at the head of a great number of thieves or moss troopers*, and had been convicted at the Assizes at Newcastle upon Tyne, was hanged within the west gate of that town, for returning from transportation. His execution had been hastened for fear of rescue.

> *History of Newcastle upon Tyne*, by John Brand 1789

> (*moss troopers – an old name for bands of thieves marauding around the mosses or moors of the borders of England and Scotland in the 17th and 18th centuries.)

Brown's journey to the gallows began at Durham Assizes on 28th July 1741 when he was convicted of felony and sentenced to be transported for seven years. In October he was put onto a vessel in the Tyne and reached Maryland in December. By November of the following year Brown was sighted in Northumberland and arrested. He was imprisoned at Morpeth and special payments were made to William Lowes, the county gaoler, to have extra guards at the gaol to watch Brown and the many other prisoners held at the time. Despite those arrangements, an unsuccessful attempt was made in the spring of 1743 by Brown and other prisoners to escape. In the first week of August 1743 William Brown appeared at the Northumberland Assizes at Newcastle.

The problem for all trials against people accused of returning unlawfully from transportation was one of satisfactory identification. Brown was identified by a master mariner named Matthias Giles. When found guilty, Brown begged to be transported again, but was sentenced to hang.

Reports in the *Newcastle Courant* one week earlier showed that Brown's wife Mary White, alias Brown, had appeared at the Newcastle Assizes at the Guildhall Newcastle upon Tyne and had been convicted of stealing and sentenced to be transported for seven years.

The execution of William Brown and the transportation of his wife did not mark the end of criminal activity by the Brown family. Forty-four years later in August 1787 the Browns appeared in the Hue and Cry columns of the *Courant*.

GENERAL HUE AND CRY

On Wednesday morning last, the 8th inst., about two o'clock a man who called himself John Thompson, whose real name is supposed to be Brown, and is said to be the son of the late infamous Sir William Brown, run away from his habitation in this town, where he resided only about half a year, and left his rent and many other debts he had contracted here, unpaid, he took with him, his wife, a son aged about 13, and two daughters, one about 15 and the other about 10 years old, a cart loaded with his House and Shop Goods, the Shop Goods consisted of Linen and Woollen Cloths, Manchester Goods, Scotch Threads, &c. He is between 50 or 60 years old, of a brown complexion, brown hair, mixed with grey, has a dark look, is strong made, lowers with his shoulders, and frequently wears a plush coat.

Newcastle Courant Saturday 18th August 1787

One of the ships used to transport convicts to America was the *Jenny* of Newcastle. Her journeys, commanded by Captain Blagdon, were reported by the *Journal*, revealing details of ocean crossing times in the 18th century.

The Jenny, Captain Blagdon, mentioned in the Journal January 25th to have sailed from this port for Virginia, with the Convicts from Durham, Northumberland and this Town, on board and also 20 indentured servants, arrived, all well, after a long Voyage of eleven weeks, having for some days before she arrived been put on short allowance.

Newcastle Journal Saturday 21st June 1766

The Jenny, Captain Blagdon, who sailed with the convicts, from this Town and the Counties of Northumberland Durham on 23rd January last for Virginia, arrived safe from thence at Portsmouth on 28th Ult., in the short passage of 22 days.

Newcastle Journal Saturday September 6th, 1766

Twelve months later the *Jenny* was on her travels again with convicts, plus some indentured servants, one of whom had a chequered history.

The Jenny, Blagdon, for Virginia, sailed on Thursday. She has on board the convicts from Durham, Morpeth and this town, and about 12 indented servants. One of the indented servants, we hear, who formerly belonged to this town, has enlisted into 46 different Regiments, been whipped out of 19, sentenced to be shot six times, but reprieved, confined in 73 different gaols under the character of Quack Doctor in seven Kingdoms, and now is only in the 32nd year of his age.

Newcastle Journal, Saturday 14th February 1767

The following year the *Gentleman's Magazine* of May 1768 carried a story which shows that the journey's of convict ships across the Atlantic were not always swift and without incident.

> The Rodney with the last cargo of convicts for Maryland having met with stormy weather on the American coast, was forced to bear away for Antigua. When the poor wretches arrived at that island they were in the most deplorable condition, full of sores, almost starved and covered with vermine, eleven had perished for want, and those that remained had eaten their shoes &c. to sustain life; add to this that the ship being leaky, they had actually lain in water a part of the voyage.
>
> *Gentleman's Magazine* May 1768

The American War of Independence (1776-1783) put an end to transporting convicts across the Atlantic Ocean. The interim solution was the Criminal Law Act of 1776, better known as the Hulks Act. This act authorised ships fitted out as prisons to be moored on the Thames to hold convicts originally sentenced to be transported overseas, and put them to hard labour cleaning out the Thames. This new system was put under the control of one of the transportation contractors, Duncan Campbell. He first had two ships, the *Justitia* and the *Censor*. The *Justitia* had previously made several voyages across the Atlantic with cargoes of convicts. John Howard had found the death rate among prisoners on the *Justitia* alarming. From August 1776, when the convicts were first put on board, to March 26, 1778, 176 out of 632 had died.

Other places to transport prisoners were looked at carefully. A site was identified on the Gambia River on the West coast of Africa. Then the authorities focussed on Australia and decided to set up what was to become virtually an open prison, a penal colony at Botany Bay. The environment was so remote and hostile that escape was virtually impossible and survival was the first priority.

Transporting convicts to America took as little as 22 days to cross the Atlantic. The convicts and their guards bound for New South Wales faced six months and more at sea before reaching Botany Bay. The first three voyages with convicts, 1787, 1789 and 1791 have become known as the First, Second and Third Fleets, although the vessels did not necessarily sail or keep together on the journeys.

The First Fleet of convict ships to Australia consisted of two escort ships, HMS *Sirius* and HMS *Supply*, three store ships *Borrowdale*, *Fishburn* and *Golden Grove* and six convict ships *Alexander*, *Charlotte*, *Scarborough*, *Prince of Wales*, *Friendship* and *Lady Penrhyn*; the last named carried female convicts. The fleet was led by Captain Arthur Phillip, who was commissioned as the first Governor of New

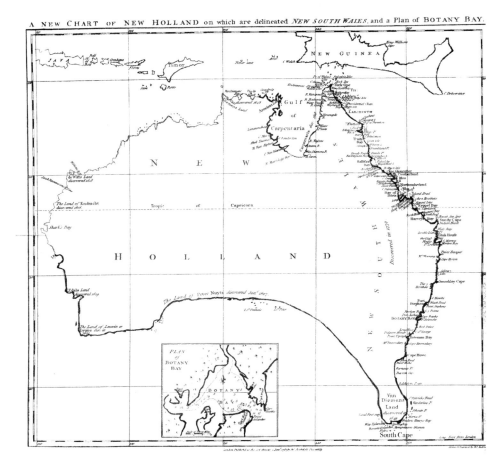

Australia, or New Holland as it was known, from Stockdale's map., 1787.

South Wales. There were 717 convicts, including 180 women, on board the ships. The fleet sailed from Portsmouth on 13th May 1787 and travelled via the Canary Islands, Rio De Janeiro, Brazil, Table Bay, South Africa to Australia and arrived at Botany Bay on 10th January 1788. Forty-eight convicts died during the journey. It was decided to establish the colony at Port Jackson, now Sydney Harbour.

On Thursday 7th February 1788 there was a parade at Port Jackson for the formal reading of the commissions, the documents of authority for the establishment and government of the new colony. Then the Governor turned to the convicts and harangued them, telling them that he was thoroughly convinced that many of them were incorrigible, and that nothing but severity would induce them to behave prop-

A detail from A Voyage to Botany Bay *by George Barrington, 1793.*

erly in the future. He also assured them that if they attempted to get into the women's tents of a night the guards would fire on them, that stealing the most trifling piece of stock or provisions was punishable by death. He anticipated only too well that were going to be severe problems with food and shelter for the colony and the behaviour of many of the convicts.

Amongst the First Fleet convicts was Elizabeth Hall from Newcastle, sentenced to seven years. There were also eleven convicts from Durham. Elizabeth Hall, said in the local newspapers to be the wife of William Hall, mariner, had been convicted for petit larceny. One list of convicts has Hall recorded as 18 years of age

What is loosely called the Second Fleet of convict ships did not sail as a group but arrived in Australia in the same month. The movement of the convicts was now fully in the charge of the convict contractor Duncan Campbell. The *Lady Juliana*, carrying female convicts sailed on 29th July 1789 and arrived 3rd June 1790. HMS *Guardian* sailed 12th September 1789 but struck an iceberg 1,300 miles from the Cape Of Good Hope and sank on 22nd December 1789. This loss was a grievous blow to the new colony. HMS *Guardian* was loaded with essential supplies for the people there who were in deep distress from want of food resources and such things as tools and implements. Three convict ships, the *Neptune, Surprise* and *Scarborough* sailed on 19th January 1790, The *Surprise* arrived on 26th June and the other two vessels arrived on the 28th June 1790. The conditions for the journey were atrocious. Out of 1,038 convicts who embarked, 278 died during the journey giving rise to the name the 'Death Fleet' for this group of ships. Several children were born on the *Lady Juliana* during the journey – not all survived. The convicts included three from Durham, and eight from Northumberland.

The Third Fleet sailed in 1791 and arrived at New South Wales in the autumn. The ships carried 2,000 convicts of whom 194 males and four females died during the voyage.

There were, amongst these cargoes of convicts, 15 men and two women sentenced by the Durham courts and 22 men and two women sentenced by the Northumberland and Newcastle courts. The women convicts in the Third Fleet included Jane Stephenson, the pickpocket, 'an old offender', who was caught red-handed in the old Moot Hall picking a pocket during a murder trial in 1790 (see page 24).

In 1791 it was announced in the *Newcastle Courant* that the wife of one of the convicts in the first three fleets to Australia had found the means to follow her husband. There was no obstacle to a wife following her convict husband provided she

Conjugal Fidelity

A female, wife to a man some since transported to New South Wales for robbing a bookseller, having the sum of £2000 lately left her by a relation, has engaged herself as a passenger to that settlement.

Newcastle Courant Saturday 31st December 1791

could pay her way, but there were hardly any examples because of the cost.

Wednesday (i.e. June 6th) one John Innes, a cartman, was committed to Newgate, to take his trial at the ensuing Assizes on suspicion of stealing several sacks of flour from a warehouse on the Quayside, the locks of which had been forced open.

Newcastle Courant Saturday 9th June , 1792

In June 1792 a tale of transportation began with a short report in the *Courant*.

Innes remained in Newgate and duly appeared at the Newcastle Assizes on Monday 6th August 1792, charged with stealing the four sacks of flour. Innes did not actually go to trial, but there were other charges outstanding against him because 'Innes on particular circumstances was ordered to find bail for his appear-

> At the General Quarter Sessions of the Peace, held at the Guildhall in this town, ... John Innes, Cartman, convicted of petit larceny, in stealing in a wherry lying at the quayside, a cag,* containing 4 gallons of spirituous liquor, sentenced to be transported beyond the seas for seven years.
>
> *Newcastle Courant* 19th January 1793
>
> (* 'cag' an old word for a cask or keg.)

ance at the next Assizes.' Long before the next Assizes however, Innes was ordered for transportation.

There was however, a hitch, proving how desperate convicts were to avoid transportation. Innes and four other convicts had been taken from Newcastle to Shields and confined on board ship for the voyage south. Somehow three of them found a way to escape. Two were retaken the same night, but Innes was on the run for three days. He was eventually found at Gateshead, disguised as a woman.

Even women convicts would fight hard to avoid transportation even to the extent of escaping from gaol. The Assize judge was merciful in the case of Sarah White who escaped from Newgate while under sentence of transportation in 1804. She was caught and sentenced to death, but later reprieved and sentenced to 14 years transportation. Two years later she was taken to Australia on a ship called the *William Pitt*.

John Sykes transcribed from local newspapers another desperate escape from Newgate in 1807 by convicts awaiting transportation, the prisoners on this occasion seem to have planned their escape with great care and have gone to endless trouble in concealing their intentions. They were not deterred even by irons and a wall about four feet thick and do not appear to have been seen nor heard of again.

December 29th 1807

Three desperate offenders John Willis, John Blakelock and David Miller first on charge of forgery, others on sentence of transportation escaped from Newgate, broke through a wall a yard and quarter thick, everything appeared normal at last time of inspection and locking up by turnkey, orderly secure, fetters appeared secure, no flaw observable in the wall, appears fragments of the wall had 'artfully' been put into place to elude detection between visits of the turnkey, the fetters had been cut asunder by implements conveyed to them, blankets by which they ascended were found upon a dunghill below.

Local Records or Historical Register of Remarkable Events, John Sykes, 1833

Transportation to Australia from the North East courts carried on in full flow in the early part of the 19th century. For example, a transcription of court records for the Northumberland and Durham Family History Society revealed that between October 1818 and January 1831 there were 50 prisoners, including 16 women, sentenced to be transported at the Newcastle upon Tyne Quarter Sessions, for the most part for petty stealing (*Journal of the Northumberland and Durham FHS* Autumn 1991). By the middle of the 19th century the tide of opinion was running against transportation as a means of dealing with criminals, and for most purposes the practice was abolished by the Penal Servitude Act of 1857. Transportation lingered on for a narrow class of convicts until, according to Robert Hughes (*The Fatal Shore* by Robert Hughes, Collins Harvill, 1987), the last shipload of convicts was discharged at Freemantle in Western Australia on 19th January 1868.

7 Dissected and Anatomized

And be it furthered enacted that ... (after execution) the body of such murderer shall ... be immediately conveyed by the Sheriff ... to the Hall of the Surgeons Company ... and the body shall be dissected and anatomized by the said Surgeons.

An Act for Better Preventing the Horrid Crime of Murder 1752

In the 18th century there was deep public anxiety about the activities of that twilight fraternity known as the 'body snatchers.' The Murder Act of 1752, to a limited extent, allayed public fears about the graves of their loved ones by permitting the judges to order the bodies of some executed murderers to be passed to local surgeons for medical research. The central thrust of this new law, however, was a final degradation of the body of the murderer after death either by public gibbeting or dissection by the surgeons. The act provided a meagre supply of bodies to meet the growing demands and enquiring minds of the medical profession.

Of the 54 people executed at Berwick, Northumberland and Newcastle in the 18th century, 15 were convicted of murder and of those two were gibbeted and the bodies of the seven listed below were ordered to be delivered to the surgeons for dissection.

1752 Ewen Macdonald for the murder of Robert Parker at the Bigg Market, Newcastle upon Tyne.

1754 Dorothy Catenby for the murder of her illegitimate child at Newcastle upon Tyne.

1764 George Stewart for the murder of Robert Lindsay at Newcastle upon Tyne.

1790 Thomas Watson for the murder of George Gibson at Newham, Northumberland.

1792 Jane Clarke and Eleanor Clarke for the murder of Margaret Crozier at The Raw Elsdon, Northumberland.

1795 Thomas Nicholson for the murder of Thomas Purvis at the Town Moor Races, Newcastle upon Tyne.

The formal association of the surgeons on Tyneside was known as the Incorporated Company of Barber Surgeons, Wax and Tallow Chandlers and Periwig Makers and they were based at the Barber Surgeons' Hall at Manors, Newcastle. The surgeons were required to dissect and anatomise the bodies of these executed criminals in public and lecture on their findings.

The Barber Surgeons' Hall at Newcastle was in Manors, at a right angle to the front of the Holy Jesus Hospital and across the land where City Road now passes in front of the hospital. The original building of 1648 was rebuilt by the company in 1730.

The first murderer at Newcastle to be sentenced under the new Act, Ewen (or Owen) Macdonald, was a young Scottish soldier convicted of murder and destined to become known in Newcastle folklore as 'Half-hanged Macdonald.'

In May 1752 companies of General Guise's Regiment (the 6th Regiment of Foot) were performing military exercises and a review on the Town Moor. Amongst those soldiers was 19 year old Ewen Macdonald. He was originally from Redcastle in Ross and Cromarty and was a brand new recruit to the Regiment having recently left military service in Holland. He was quartered in the Bigg Market at the Black Bull Inn. The following Wednesday the *Newcastle Gazette* carried a report on the exercises as well as a report of a tragedy in the Bigg Market.

Macdonald had fallen into an argument with some fellow drinkers in the Black Bull. One of them was Robert Parker, a cooper from Newcastle. Words soon turned to blows, and Macdonald stabbed Parker in the neck. According to one report, he

The Barber Surgeons' Hall.

also broke the arm of another man. Piecing together the story from contemporary accounts it seems probable that the fatal fight took place in High Bridge.

Macdonald appeared at the Newcastle Assizes, was convicted and sentenced to death. According to normal practice, Macdonald would be hanged the next day but one after sentence, but the judge ordered a respite of sentence for several weeks. His reason is not clear and no formal explanation was ever published. However orders finally came through for the execution to carried out rather later than the original date.

During this waiting time, Macdonald was held in Newgate Gaol in solitary confinement as required by the Murder Act. He was closely attended by the gaol chaplain the Rev. Mr Wilkinson. A broadsheet entitled *The Dying Words and Confession of Owen Macdonald* was published immediately after the execution and it appears to have been prepared in advance of death as a personal statement rather than the usual account of the crime. The text did not describe Macdonald's behaviour at the gallows and the broadsheet also thanked people who had tried to obtain a reprieve for him. This is one explanation for the stay or respite of the date of execution. The broadsheet is written in the first person but the text is not the language of a young, rough, inexperienced and uneducated soldier. It must have been written on Macdonald's behalf by the gaol chaplain the Rev. Mr. Wilkinson. That was a common enough practice.

In his confession, Macdonald described the crime:

> **Being at Supper by the Kitchen Fire in my Quarters, the sign of the Black Bull in the Big-market, two men came in for a Pint of Beer, who were both of them unknown to me; the one of them (a Thing as I have since been informed, generally practiced by him) passed several opprobrious Reflections upon me, which I very patiently heard, till I was upbraided with my native Country, Scotland, then actuated by the Fury of an ungovernable Passion, I arose from my Supper, and in the Heigth of this Passion followed him into the Entry when I struck at one, with the Knife.**

Unfortunately, Macdonald did not strike the man who had been goading him, but his companion. Macdonald claimed he was not even aware of having the knife in his hand at the time.

The town hangman in 1752 was John Young. He had some difficulty in hanging Ewen Macdonald on Thursday 28th September. The *Newcastle Courant* said that Macdonald's 'Behaviour in endeavouring to throw the executioner from off the ladder was unbecoming one just on the brink of eternity; however it was generally and justly believed that he had been grossly irritated to the perpetration of the Crime for which he suffered his unhappy end was pitied by everyone.'

His body was cut down and delivered to the Barber Surgeons for dissection.

> **That afternoon the public Dissection of the body of the Criminal, with lectures thereon, in pursuance of the late Act of Parliament, was finished at the Surgeons Hall, the Lecturers were Mr Hallowell, Mr Stodart, Mr Greenwell and Mr Lambert. Mr Hallowell exhibited all the Bones of the Body and Abdominal Viscera. Mr Stodart the Manner of Nature converting our ailment into Blood with a description of its circulation. Mr Greenwell the parts belonging to Generation and the Eye; and Mr Lambert the Muscular Parts of the whole Body: all which were executed with the greatest accuracy and very much to the Advantage of the younger gentlemen of the faculty.**
>
> *Newcastle Courant* Saturday October 14th 1752

One of the interesting things about these reports is there is not a hint that anything unusual may have occurred with the body of Macdonald after he had been left hanging for the usual hour or so and then transferred to the Barber Surgeons' Hall. Examples occurred around the country of criminals recovering on the surgeon's table after execution and the newspapers had no compunction about publishing details.

The next history of Newcastle upon Tyne written by John Brand in 1789, 37 years after the execution of Macdonald, simply carries a short note that in 1752 'a soldier was condemned for murder and hanged on the 28th September following.' John Baillie, in his history of 1801, did not mention the Macdonald case. Eneas Mackenzie in 1827 and Thomas Oliver in 1831, record Macdonald's crime and execution, but none these sources report anything unusual happening at the Barber Surgeons' Hall.

In 1833, 81 years after the execution, John Sykes published his *Local Records or Historical Register of Remarkable Events*, consisting of two volumes of stories of events in Northumberland, Durham and Tyneside over several centuries. The more recent material consisted of transcripts from local newspapers. The first part of his account of the story of Macdonald is simply an amalgam of the *Courant* reports of May, September and October 1752. But then appears for the first time in print a report that Macdonald had begun to recover in the Barber Surgeons' Hall after his execution and been dispatched by a young surgeon wielding a wooden mallet.

> It was said that after the body was taken to the Surgeons' Hall, and placed ready for dissection, that the surgeons were called to attend a case at the Infirmary, who on their return. found Macdonald so far recovered as to be sitting up; He immediately begged for mercy, but a young surgeon not wishing to be disappointed of the dissection, seized a wooden mall with which he deprived him of his life. It was further reported, as just vengeance of God, that this young man was soon after killed in the stable by his own horse. They showed a mallet at the Surgeons' Hall as the identical one used by the surgeon. I have thrown this note together from the report current some years ago, but which is now fast dying away.

Sykes's final line hints at some reservations about the accuracy of the tale. He would know that there was nothing in the newspapers of the day to support the story. But it was a potent legend, arousing vivid images of this young Scot recovering from his ordeal only to be put to death on the dissection table. Sykes's story was repeated word-for-word, but without the last sentence, forty years later in a list of 'Executions which have taken place in Newcastle since 1306', published in Chater's *Diary and Local Remembrancer* 1873. In the version published in the *Monthly*

Chronicle in 1887 the expression 'Half-hanged Macdonald' appears for the first time with many inaccuracies and much dramatic embellishment. Macdonald's regiment had become the 42nd Royal Highlanders (the Black Watch, who actually were in Ireland at that time), he was supposedly attired in full highland dress, and the knife he used was now referred to as a 'corc', 'sgiandhu' or a gully knife, when in fact it was simply the knife he had used to eat his supper. The story concludes with the Sykes' story of Macdonald recovering in the dissection room only to be felled by a young surgeon using a wooden mallet. This dramatic version of events has been repeated as established fact in many books about Newcastle since that time and the remarkable legend will probably continue. But there is nothing about Macdonald's alleged recovery in contemporary local newspapers or in the minutes of the Barber Surgeon' Company. There is no record, in the years following the execution of Macdonald, of any person let alone a 'young surgeon' being kicked to death in a stable by his horse.

There was, of course, a problem about a sufficient supply of bodies for the medical profession to use for teaching and research. The execution of condemned murderers did not provide an abundant supply of bodies for the surgeons in the North East. In the half century 1750-1800 the average was about one every eight years. There was great public alarm about the activities of body snatchers. The infamous William Burke was hanged at Edinburgh on 27th January 1829 for murder committed in the course of his activities in providing bodies to sell to the surgeons. His equally infamous colleague William Hare escaped trial himself by giving evidence against Burke and he died free but in poverty.

The North East was caught up in this dreadful trade and disturbing things occurred. Between September 1825 and January 1826 three bodies were found in transit through Newcastle to Edinburgh. Disgusting smells from strange packages led to shocking discoveries and in 1828 two more female bodies were found in transit. All the stories were picked up by John Sykes from the local newspapers.

September 16th 1825

About half past ten o'clock at night, a person having the appearance of a porter, brought a travelling trunk to the Turf Hotel coach office in Collingwood Street, Newcastle where it was left for the purpose of being forwarded the following morning to Edinburgh. The address it bore was 'James Syme Esq, 6 Forth Street, Edinburgh' but in consequence of its having been deposited in that part of the office where packages were placed for the south west coach, and no coaches going north on Sunday, it was detained until the Monday, when a most nauseous smell was felt from a liquid oozing therefrom. When the trunk was opened by order of the magistrates, it was found to contain the body of a young woman supposed to be about 19 years of age, of fair complexion, light eyes and yellow hair, and without marks of violence. The body after a coroners inquest was interred

January 6th 1826

A large box arrived in Newcastle in the night by the Telegraph coach from Leeds weighing upwards of sixteen stones. Suspicion having been excited by similar boxes having passed through Newcastle, the officers of police were sent for, and on opening the box, they discovered the dead body of a man whose stature must have exceeded six feet. He was apparently between forty and fifty years of age, large boned with dark hair and aquiline nose. The corpse had not become putrid. The package was addressed to 'Mr Simpson, 61 Princes Street, Edinburgh'. A coroner's inquest was held on this subject on the following morning and a verdict returned that 'no marks of violence appear on the body, but by what means he came by his death, no evidence doth appear'. The body was afterwards interred.

January 15th 1826

The dead body of a man was discovered in a common deal box brought from beyond York, to the Turf Hotel coach-office in Collingwood Street, Newcastle, for Edinburgh. It was interred at the Ballast Hills.

November 10th 1828

The dead bodies of two females were discovered in the coach office of the Turf

Hotel in Newcastle. One came by the Highflyer coach from York, and the other was brought by a man to be booked for Edinburgh. In consequence of suspicions a police officer was sent for, and the man was taken into custody. The packages were directed to different parties in Edinburgh. Inquests were held the following day by the coroner for Newcastle, and no marks of violence appearing on the bodies, the verdict was to that effect, and they were interred in St Johns' churchyard. The package from York came to Newcastle first on the 8th and being suspected returned thither; and the coach proprietors at York sent it back by the same coach. The man who took the other box to the coach office was tried and acquitted.

Inquests were necessary, of course, on each occasion. Events of this kind stoked up public anxiety and various strategies were tried to defeat the grave robbers; heavy grave stones requiring block and tackle to move them, or iron cages around the grave. The challenge was to keep the grave intact long enough for the body to become unfit for use by the surgeons. Another tactic was to build a watch tower in a cemetery to provide shelter for a family or well trusted paid guardians to keep a watch on the grave. There is a famous example in Morpeth Cemetery. Public anxiety could also reach something approaching riot proportions in certain cases, at Berwick upon Tweed for example in 1792.

BERWICK

A rumour having prevailed among the lower classes of the inhabitants of Berwick, that three young surgeons of that place made a practice of procuring the bodies of persons recently interred in the churchyard there, for the purpose of dissecting them, an alarming mob assembled on Tuesday, proceeded to the utmost violence and totally demolished a building belonging to Mr Nesbit where they found several dead bodies; they also attempted to effect the like purpose on another house belonging to a person whom they supposed to be concerned in the robbery of the sacred sepulchres of their friends. This violent disposition of the populace called forth the utmost exertions of the magistracy; the Riot Act was read without effect, and to their aid they were under the necessity of calling forth the troops from the garrison before the tumultuous mob could be induced to disperse. Mr Miller is lodged in prison, Mr Yellowley is out on bail, and a reward of ten guineas is offered for apprehending Mr Nesbit who has absconded. Great praise is due to Mr Mayor and the other magistrates for the great activity and prudent methods put in practice on this occasion.

Newcastle Chronicle Saturday August 11th 1792

The biography of Billy Purvis, the 19th century entertainer, revealed that he came across a very similar incident in his travels in 1824.

(Describing the movements of Billy Purvis, late summer 1824)

Going to Berwick he next visited Coldingham and Alemouth. "I next proceeded to Coldingham, and as I was leaving Alemouth, I was stopped by a crowd of persons assembled round a carrier's cart or wagon, and being curious to know the cause of the gathering, I found that a long box, among other goods in the wagon, labelled, 'Surgeon, Edinburgh.' was discovered to send forth a most unsavoury odour, and attracted the attention of the carrier's wife. She was not long in expressing her opinion that something 'no cannie' was in the box; and others hearing her words, strengthened her suspicions by affirming that she was right. A hole was made, and a piece of wire poked in and drawn out, bearing with it evident signs of far gone putrefaction. The wife insisted on her husband breaking open the box, which operation was performed, when lo! no sooner was the lid removed than the putrid corpse of a poor old woman who had died a week before, was discovered in the box. The carrier informed the people who had given him the box to carry and no sooner was the recreant's name uttered than away ran the crowd to give the doctor the benefit of 'Lynch Law'. The inhuman exhuming son of Celsus was found in a low thatched cottage, which the infuriated villagers attacked. A constable was sent for and, as he did not deny the charge, he was taken to prison. His accomplice (a young surgeon) escaped; and the body of the puir auld wife was again buried."

Extract from *The Life of Billy Purvis (1784-1853)* published by T. Arthur of Newcastle 1875

The Anatomy Act of 1832 finally provided proper control of anatomy schools by inspection and established regulations for the legal provision of bodies for use by the medical profession Problems with grave robbers rumbled on into Victorian times but public anxiety was diminishing as the act was seen establish a more professional and acceptable practice.

8 A Policeman's Lot

An Act for Lighting the Streets, Maintaining a Regular Nightly Watch within the Town of Newcastle upon Tyne and Regulating Coachmen, Chairmen &c, 1763

'... there shall be a sufficient number of able-bodied men, not exceeding Fifty in Whole, appointed from Time to Time, as the said Commissioners, or any Seven of them think proper, to watch within the Walls of the said Town of Newcastle upon Tyne every night from the twenty-ninth Day of September to twenty-fifth day of March each year'.

In the absence of professional police forces, the 18th century system for investigating crimes was largely a 'do it yourself' arrangement. The injured party and the community, through the parish leaders and locally appointed constables, banded together to recover stolen goods and seize suspected offenders to bring them before a justice for examination and committal to prison. In Newcastle there was an additional resource of police in the form of the 'Sergeants at Mace.' The origin of these officers of the town lies in the charter of 1400. According to Eneas Mackenzie, writing in 1827, the quality of these officers varied from time to time.

> The mace was anciently a heavy weapon, used by cavalry or ecclesiastics, who were not permitted to carry swords. It is now a highly ornamented emblem of the authority of the chief officer of a corporate body, before whom it is carried on state occasions. The annual salary of this officer is £5. There are eight sergeants at mace, including the water bailiff and sheriff's sergeant. Seven of these sergeants constitute the police establishment of the town, and are paid £225 per annum. They are occasionally assisted by the constables of the twenty-four wards of the town. The present sergeants at

mace are Matthew Gilpatrick (sheriff's sergeant), James Atkin, Joseph Wake, Charles Sloan, Joshua Elliott, Thomas Barkas and John Lough. Formerly, little attention was paid to age activity, or intelligence, in the choice of sergeants, who were, in general, ill qualified to discharge the arduous duties of their office. To remedy this defect, Mr Forsyth, a non-commissioned officer in the Northumberland militia, was selected to re-organise the police of the town; and by his acuteness, promptitude and courage, it has become little inferior to the best establishments of the kind in London.

A Descriptive and Historical Account of the Town and County of Newcastle upon Tyne by Eneas Mackenzie, 1827

The sergeant at mace, Thomas Forsyth, mentioned by Mackenzie, appears to have been an efficient police or peace officer. In 1823 he was presented with a silver cup 'by several drapers in Newcastle, for his exertions as a police officer in that town.'

The County Winter Assizes of 1930-31. The visitong judge is flanked by the Sword Bearer and, on the right, the Mace Bearer.

The Lamp and Watch Act of 1763 permitted the formation of a night watch within the town walls and this service was later extended outside the walls. Eneas Mackenzie described the night watch as a force of 26 watchmen, under the direction of a constable, known as Captain of the Watch, assisted by two night constables. They kept watch from 10pm until 6am, making rounds and calling out the time every half hour. Each watchman was provided with a warm watch coat, a lantern, a rattle and a stick with an iron hook at one end. They were paid half a guinea per week, with a one guinea bonus at the end of the season if they had behaved well. Outside the walls there were 30 watchmen including two governors.

The need to pay a gratuity for good behaviour raises a question mark about the effectiveness of this force. Mackenzie recorded that the watchmen were paid one shilling for each arrest which, almost inevitably, led to problems.

> On Wednesday some young men who were enquiring into the cause of an affray at the Head of the Side, were very improperly seized by a constable and carried to the Close-gate prison, where they were confined all night. On stating the matter to the sitting magistrate next morning, the constable was severely reprimanded and informed that the commission of similar breaches of duty would be punished with exemplary vigour.
>
> *The Newcastle Chronicle or Weekly Advertizer* Saturday 23rd February 1793

Mackenzie was scathing about the watch, 'The night police is wretchedly conducted, and outrages have been frequently committed that have strongly excited the public indignation.' Four years before Mackenzie's history was published there had been a great fuss at Newcastle upon Tyne about the conduct of the watch. In 1823 a man named Thomas Waller Watson brought an action against Thomas Carr, who was then Captain of the Watch, for false imprisonment. Watson and a friend named Walton had passed the evening in Newcastle with two acquaintances. In the street they became separated a short distance and one had called to the other using a phrase from a well known song, the other replied in similar fashion. For that conduct Watson and Walton were seized by three watchmen and brought before Thomas Carr, accused of causing an affray. The captain chose to believe his watchmen and Watson and Walton were detained some 12 hours. When the action for false imprisonment was brought, Carr, who had already lost his job, was ordered to pay both Watson and Walton 40 shillings damages plus costs. This fine meant that Carr went straight to Newgate Gaol as an insolvent debtor.

Mackenzie's final comment was generous and understanding, 'Mr Carr and the other watchmen who receive one shilling for every person they lay hold of in the streets, are not so much to blame. It is the system that is bad.'

Clearly 'Canny Newcastle' needed something better than this to enforce the law and so did the rest of the country. The wind of change of was blowing through the criminal justice system as one century ended the next began. The first police force for Newcastle was formed in 1832 but disbanded a year later. The public did not like the new system. However, legislation required the county boroughs to set up a professional police force. The Newcastle authorities sought out the best practice and finally the Newcastle Borough Police began to patrol the town on 2nd May 1836. Leading them towards the enormous changes and demands of the future was the first Chief Constable John Stephens, and here to mark the end of one era and the beginning of the next is one of those constables (pictured in later life) the aptly named John Hope.

Police Constable John Hope photographed c.1860.

9 Executions 1700-1919

Executions at Berwick upon Tweed, Newcastle upon Tyne and Northumberland 1700-1919
(Some military executions following court martial are included)

1701 **Leggerton**, Thomas, a wheelwright, hanged at Newcastle upon Tyne on Thursday 25th September 1701 for stabbing a young man to death. He was buried in St Andrew's churchyard.

Fenwick (Fenweik), John, JP, of Rock in Northumberland, hanged near the scene of his crime in Newgate Street, Newcastle upon Tyne on Thursday 25th September 1701 for the murder of Ferdinando Foster M.P. of Bamburgh. This execution was said to have been either from a thorn tree near to the White Cross (a market cross) or from a piece of timber placed between the gaoler's house and Newgate Gaol.

1733 **Tweddle**, (Tweddal) John, and **Morrison**, Bartholomew. Offences unknown, hanged on the Town Moor at Newcastle upon Tyne on Monday 13th August 1733.

These were the first executions at Newcastle since 1701. Possibly there was a policy to increase the number of prisoners transported. The newspapers took note:

> It is observed that there has not been a Person hanged in Newcastle these thirty Years last past.
>
> *Newcastle Courant* Saturday August 18th 1733

1739 **Curry**, Michael, hanged at Westgate, Newcastle upon Tyne at 8am on Wednesday 5th September 1739 for the murder of Robert Shevill, landlord of the Three Horseshoes Inn at Hartley Northumberland. His body was gibbeted at the point opposite St Mary's Island, close to Whitley Bay and in sight of the scene of his crime just across the bay from Hartley. (Part of a double execution see below.) A commemorative plaque now stands on the headland at the beginning of the causeway leading to St Mary's Island Whitley Bay to mark the spot where the gibbet was erected. The headland has since 1739 been known as Curry's Point.

Wilson, John, hanged at Westgate, Newcastle upon Tyne on Wednesday 5th September 1739 for the murder of Barbara Trumble of Dunclawood and buried in St John's churchyard, Newcastle upon Tyne.

Smith, William, hanged on the Town Moor at Newcastle upon Tyne on Friday 14th September 1739 for the murder of his wife. He was 53 years of age.

1740 **Clarkson**, James, a notorious thief and housebreaker, hanged at Berwick upon Tweed 19th November 1740.

1742 **Todd**, John, and **Simpson**, William, hanged at Morpeth on Friday 24th September 1742 for sheep-stealing.

1743 **Brown**, William, hanged at Westgate, Newcastle upon Tyne on Monday 8th August 1743 a border thief returning unlawfully from transportation. He was commonly known as 'Sir William Brown'. Soldiers were used at the execution to prevent rescue.

1744 **Lister**, Thomas for horse-stealing, two black mares, and **Maben**, James and **Samuel**, John for coining, a triple execution, all three hanged at Westgate, Newcastle upon Tyne on Saturday 11th August 1744. At the same Assize, John Windram and Alexander Kerr for aiding and abetting Maben to escape from gaol were sentenced to be transported for seven years. Maben and Samuel were at first ordered to be hung, drawn and quartered (the usual sentence for coining – a form of treason), but that sentence was reduced to being drawn to the gallows on a hurdle then death by hanging.

1746 **Lewis** (a Welsh soldier) and **Baillie** (an Irish soldier) – Deserting the King's army – Shot at Berwick upon Tweed on 16th June 1746.

Stewart, John, hanged at Morpeth on Wednesday 3rd September 1746 for burglary and horse stealing at Castlegarth, Newcastle upon Tyne (i.e. Northumberland county land).

Anthony, Alexander, a soldier, in Brigadier Cholmondely's Regiment, aged 23 years, shot on the Town Moor at Newcastle upon Tyne on Monday 15th September 1746 for desertion.

1747 **Maccan**, George, shot at Berwick upon Tweed on 6th February 1747 for desertion. A soldier in General Guise's Regiment of Foot; deserted four times, once to the rebel army.

1751 **Brown**, Richard, hanged on the Town Moor at Newcastle upon Tyne on

Wednesday 21st August 1751 for the murder of his daughter. A keel-man aged 58 years. Brown was visited in the Newgate Gaol at Newcastle upon Tyne by Charles Wesley.

1752 **Macdonald**, Ewen, a soldier aged 19 years, hanged on the Town Moor at Newcastle upon Tyne on Thursday 28th September 1752 for the murder of Robert Parker in the Bigg Market, Newcastle upon Tyne. The body of Macdonald was sent to the Barber Surgeons' Hall at Manors, Newcastle upon Tyne upon Tyne for public dissection. He has become known as 'Half-hanged Macdonald' because of a legend that about an hour later he was seen to sit up in the dissecting room of the Surgeons' Hall and was then hit with a mallet by a young surgeon to finish off the executioner's task.

1754 **Catenby**, Dorothy, a widow, hanged on the Town Moor at Newcastle upon Tyne on Monday 19th August 1754 for the murder of her illegitimate child. Her body was sent to the Barber Surgeons' Hall for public dissection.

1758 **Bland**, William, a soldier, shot on the Town Moor at Newcastle upon Tyne on Monday 20th February 1758 for desertion.

Drydon, Margaret, hanged at Berwick upon Tweed on Wednesday 3rd May 1758 for the murder of her illegitimate child.

Williamson, Alice, aged 68 years, hanged on the Town Moor at Newcastle upon Tyne on Monday 7th August 1758 for burglary at the Groat Market, Newcastle upon Tyne.

1761 **Patterson**, Peter, hanged at Morpeth on Tuesday 6th October 1761 for high treason by taking part in a riot at Morpeth on 2nd March 1761. When Patterson, aged 74 years, was hanged the rope broke and he was hanged a second time. In accordance with the sentence for treason his heart was cut out and burned. The body was cut on the quarters but not separated.

1764 **Stewart**, George a pawnbroker, hanged on the Town Moor at Newcastle upon Tyne on Monday 27th August 1764, for the murder of a keelman, Robert Lindsay. His body was sent to the Barber Surgeons' Hall for public dissection.

Edgar, James, hanged at Westgate, Newcastle upon Tyne on Monday 3rd September 1764 for housebreaking at the home of late Edward Bigge at West Jesmond. A cobbler of Sandgate.

1765 **Hall**, Joseph, A soldier of the 6th Regiment of Foot (General Guises) quartered at Newcastle upon Tyne. Hanged at Morpeth on Thursday 15th August 1765 for highway robbery at Gosforth.

1774 **Davidson**, George, hanged at Morpeth on Saturday 16th August 1774 for rape.

1776 **Knowles**, Robert, hanged on the Town Moor at Newcastle upon Tyne on Wednesday 21st August 1776 and buried in St Andrew's churchyard the same day. A postman convicted of stealing a letter containing two £50 bank notes.

Mackenzie, Andrew a soldier, hanged at Westgate Newcastle upon Tyne on Wednesday 21st August 1776 for robbery. His accomplice Barney Reay, another soldier, escaped from military custody and was circulated in the Hue and Cry of the local newspaper, Reay does not appear to have ever been traced.

1783 **Alexander**, William, hanged on the Town Moor at Newcastle upon Tyne on Monday 17th November 1783 for forgery and buried in St Andrew's churchyard. Sentenced on 16th August 1783 but execution delayed because of appeals on points of law. (A gentlemen had his pocket picked below the gallows during the execution.)

1784 **Chambers**, James and **Collins**, William hanged on the Town Moor at Newcastle upon Tyne on Friday 27th August 1784 for robbery and buried in the same grave in St Andrew's churchyard. The same day Chambers admitted picking three or four pockets at an execution on the same spot a few months earlier (see Alexander, William 17th November 1783 above).

1785 **Graham**, William, and **Cockburn**, William, hanged at Morpeth on Tuesday 16th August 1785 for horse stealing.

1786 **Jennings**, Henry, a yeoman, hanged on the Town Moor at Newcastle upon Tyne on Wednesday 30th August 1786, for stealing a bay gelding, and buried in St Andrew's churchyard the same day. (During the public execution a boy, Peter Donnison, was apprehended picking the pocket of a man standing near the foot of the gallows.)

1788 **Winter**, John, **Winter**, Robert, father and son respectively, hanged at Morpeth on Wednesday 6th August 1788. for housebreaking at the mansion of the Charlton family at Hesleyside, Northumberland

1789 **Young**, Thomas, hanged at Morpeth on Wednesday 26th August 1789 for highway robbery, he was 24 years of age.

1790 **Watson**, Thomas, hanged at Westgate, Newcastle upon Tyne on Thursday 5th August 1790, for the murder of George Gibson at Newham, and his body was sent to the Barber Surgeons' Hall for public dissection. (During Watson's trial at the old Moot Hall on Castle Garth, Newcastle upon Tyne, an old offender, Jane Stephenson, was caught in the act of picking a pocket in the court. She was detained and put before the judge the same day at the end of Watson's trial and sentenced to be transported for seven years.)

Brown, John (age 36 years) – Housebreaking at Fenham, **Greenwood**,* James – Shopbreaking at North Sunderland, **Bolton**, George – horse stealing – a triple execution by hanging at Morpeth on Wednesday 18th August 1790 that drew 'a multitude of spectators'.
(*Greenwood's brother and John Lord were hanged at York circa 1788)

1792 **Winter**, William, **Clarke**, Jane and **Clarke**, Eleanor, a triple hanging at Westgate, Newcastle upon Tyne on Friday 10th August 1792 for the murder of Margaret Crozier at The Raw, Elsdon Northumberland. The bodies of the two women were sent to the Barber Surgeons' Hall for public dissection. Winter's body was gibbeted on the moors to the south of Elsdon. The executioner was William Gardner a fellow prisoner sentenced to death for sheep-stealing at the same Assizes but reprieved for transportation for taking on the task of hanging Winter, Clarke and Clarke. Winter was about 24 years of age, the girls under 20 years.

Broadwater, Sylvester – stealing a mare value £20 at Brampton, **Marshall**, Joseph – stealing a mare value £10 at Brampton, and **Taylor**, Christopher – arson and robbery at Bardon Mill – a triple execution by hanging at Morpeth on Wednesday 22nd August 1792.

1793 **Clarke**, Walter, burglary and stealing clothing at Wooler, and **Dunn**, Margaret – burglary and stealing clothing, gold and silver at Corbridge – Clarke age 50 years and Dunn aged 45 years were hanged at Fair Moor, Morpeth on Wednesday 14th August 1793.

1795 **Nicholson**, Thomas, hanged on the Town Moor at Newcastle on Saturday 8th August 1795 for the murder of Thomas Purvis at Newcastle Town Moor Races. A pit-man aged 22 years, his body was sent to the Barber Surgeons' Hall for public dissection. Purvis was buried at Ballast Hills cemetery. In 1796 other men appeared at the Assizes charged with complicity in the murder but were not convicted.

1801 **Scott**, John, hanged at Morpeth on Thursday 19th November 1801 for sheep-stealing.

1805 **Clare**, Thomas hanged at Westgate, Newcastle upon Tyne on Friday August 16th 1805 for the murder of William Todd at Cullercoats. A soldier of the 2nd Staffs. Militia aged 21 years. THE LAST EXECUTION AT WESTGATE.

1808 **O'Bryan**, Martin, hanged at Morpeth on Thursday 1st September 1808 for robbery and wounding.

1809 **Boyd**, John, hanged at Morpeth on Saturday 19th August 1809, aged 20 years for forgery.

1816 **O'Neill**, James, hanged on the Town Moor at Newcastle upon Tyne on Saturday 7th September 1816, for highway robbery, and buried in St Andrew's churchyard. An Irishman aged 23 years.

1817 **Smith**, Charles, hanged on the Town Moor at Newcastle upon Tyne on Wednesday 3rd December 1817, for the murder of Charles Stuart, and his body was sent to the Barber Surgeons' Hall for public dissection. A macabre relic of the dissection has survived. A piece of Smith's skin was saved, treated and bound into a book containing details of his conviction. The book is now held in the collections of Newcastle City Library, Newcastle upon Tyne. Charles Smith was 49 years of age.

1819 **Charlton**, Joseph, hanged at Morpeth on Wednesday 14th April 1819, for an unnatural crime, aged 24 years.

1821 **Wilkinson**, John, and **Hetherington**, William Surtees, hanged at Morpeth on Monday 10th September 1821 for robbery.

1822 **Lawson**, Mark, and **Currie**, William, Northumberland – hanged at Morpeth 20th March 1822 for robbery at Gosforth.

1823 **Griffin**, Grace, hanged at Berwick upon Tweed on Saturday 26th July 1823 for the murder of her husband John Griffin. THE LAST EXECUTION AT BERWICK UPON TWEED.

1829 **Jamieson**, Jane, hanged on the Town Moor at Newcastle upon Tyne on Saturday 7th March 1829, for the murder of her mother Margaret Jamieson at the Keelmen's Hospital. Her body was sent to the Barber Surgeons' Hall for public dissection. Several persons had their pockets picked in the crowd during the execution. Jamieson, a fishwife aged 30 years, was the first prisoner to be executed from the new Newcastle Borough Gaol at Carliol Square, Newcastle upon Tyne. She was the last woman to be executed at Newcastle upon Tyne and this was the last occasion that the court ordered the body of an executed person at Newcastle upon Tyne to be delivered to the Barber Surgeons' Hall for public dissection.

1844 **Sherwood**, Mark, hanged by a Scottish executioner, Murdock of Glasgow, in the centre of the Town Moor Race Course at Newcastle upon Tyne on Friday 23rd August 1844, for the murder of his wife Ann Sherwood. The trap door platform known as the drop was used for the first time at Newcastle upon Tyne to execute Sherwood. He was buried within the precincts of the Newcastle Borough Gaol at Carliol Square. THE LAST EXECUTION ON ANY PART OF THE TOWN MOOR AT NEWCASTLE UPON TYNE.

1846 **Joicey**, Ralph, hanged at Morpeth on Thursday 26th February 1846 for the murder of his father by poisoning.

1847 **Matthews**, George – Murder of Daniel Hives, and **Welch**, James – Murder of Thomas Proud, both hanged at Morpeth on Wednesday 17th March 1847. A double public execution on top of the gate tower at Morpeth Gaol. THE LAST PUBLIC EXECUTION AT MORPETH

1850 **Forbes**, Patrick, publicly hanged by Nathaniel Howard, the York City hangman, at the north boundary wall of the Newcastle Borough Gaol facing Carliol Street, Newcastle upon Tyne on Saturday 24th August 1850, for the murder of his wife Elizabeth Forbes. 16,000 people are said to have gathered in Carliol Street to watch the execution. Aged 40 years. Buried inside the gaol.

1863 **Vass**, George, publicly hanged by Thomas Askern on top of the wall of the Borough Gaol. Newcastle upon Tyne at the foot of Carliol Square facing the steps of the Royal Arcade on Saturday 14th March 1863 for the murder of Margaret Jane

Docherty at West Walls, Newcastle upon Tyne. Aged 19 years. Buried inside the gaol. THE LAST PUBLIC EXECUTION IN NEWCASTLE UPON TYNE.

1868 THE LAST PUBLIC EXECUTION IN THE UNITED KINGDOM was at Newgate, London on Monday 26th May 1868 when Michael Barrett, a Fenian, was hanged by William Calcraft for causing an explosion at Clerkenwell prison.

1875 **Anderson**, John William, hanged by William Marwood inside the Newcastle Borough Gaol on Thursday 23rd December 1875, for the murder of his wife Elizabeth Anderson. He was 32 years of age. Buried inside the gaol.

Charlton, Richard, hanged inside Morpeth Gaol on Thursday 23rd December 1875 for the murder of his wife.

1876 **Hunter**, George hanged inside Morpeth Gaol on 28th March 1876 for the murder of a fellow workman. THE LAST EXECUTION AT MORPETH GAOL (closed on 24th October 1881)

1886 **Judge**, Patrick, hanged by James Berry and John George Morley inside H.M. Prison (formerly called the Borough Gaol) Carliol Square Newcastle upon Tyne at 8am on Tuesday 16th November 1886, for the murder of his wife. A hawker aged 48 years, he was buried inside the prison.

1890 **Row,** William, hanged by James Berry in H.M. Prison, Newcastle upon Tyne on Wednesday 12th March 1890, for the murder of co-habitee Lily M. Wilson. A shoemaker aged 40 years. Buried inside the prison.

1894 **Emery**, Samuel George, hanged by William Billington in H.M. Prison, Newcastle upon Tyne at 8am on Tuesday 11th December 1894, for the murder of Mary Ann Marshall at Tynemouth. A private in the South Staffordshire Regiment, aged 20 years, he was buried inside the prison.

1901 **Miller**, John, and **Miller**, John Robert, hanged by William Billington and John Ellis inside H.M. Prison, Newcastle upon Tyne on Saturday 7th December 1901, for the murder of Joseph Ferguson at Cullercoats. John Miller was 67 years of age and his nephew John Robert Miller 31 years, they were buried in the prison.

1905 **Perkins**, Henry, Newcastle upon Tyne, hanged by Henry Pierrepoint and John Ellis inside H.M. Prison, Newcastle upon Tyne at 8am on Wednesday 6th December

1905, for the murder of Patrick Durkin in a Newgate Street lodging-house Newcastle upon Tyne, He was 40 years of age. Buried in the prison

1910 **Dickman**, John Alexander, hanged by John Ellis and an assistant Williams on Tuesday 9th August 1910 in H.M. Prison, Newcastle upon Tyne for the murder of John Innes Nisbet on a train between Newcastle upon Tyne and Morpeth. He was 45 years of age. Buried in the prison.

1913 **Amos**, John Vickers, hanged by Thomas W. Pierrepoint and Arthur Willis at 8am on Tuesday 22nd July 1913 inside H.M. Prison, Newcastle upon Tyne for the murder of Police Sergeant Andrew Barton at Bedlington. He was 35 years of age. Buried in the prison.

1917 **Cavanagh**, William James, hanged by Thomas W. Pierrepoint and Robert Baxter inside H.M. Prison, Newcastle upon Tyne on Tuesday 18th December 1917 for the murder of Henry Arthur Hollyer at West Street, Newcastle upon Tyne. He was 29 years of age. Buried in the prison.

1919 **Scott**, Ernest Bernard, hanged inside H.M.Prison, Newcastle upon Tyne at 8am on Wednesday 26th November 1919 for the murder of Rebecca Jane Quinn at New Delaval. He was 28 years of age. Buried in the prison.

Quinn, Ambrose, hanged inside H.M. Prison, Newcastle upon Tyne at 9.15am on Wednesday 26th November 1919 for the murder of Elizabeth Ann Quinn at Hawes Street, Newcastle upon Tyne. He was 28 years of age. Buried in the prison. THE LAST PERSON TO BE EXECUTED AT NEWCASTLE UPON TYNE.

H.M. Prison, Newcastle upon Tyne closed on Tuesday 31st March 1925 and Durham Prison was then used for prisoners from Newcastle upon Tyne and Northumberland. The first execution at Durham Prison of a prisoner from Berwick upon Tweed, Newcastle upon Tyne or Northumberland was James Smith aged 23 years, hanged by Pierrepoint and Philips at Durham Prison on Tuesday 10th August 1926 for the murder, by stabbing, of his wife Catherine Smith at 6 Silver Street, Newcastle upon Tyne on Monday 26th April 1926.

Suggested Reading

Local history

The History of Newcastle upon Tyne by Henry Bourne 1736

History of Newcastle upon Tyne by John Brand 1789

An Impartial History of Newcastle upon Tyne by John Baillie, 1801

Descriptive and Historical Account of Newcastle and Gateshead by Eneas Mackenzie 1827

Newcastle Town by J.R. Charleton 1885

History of Newcastle and Gateshead by Richard Welford 1885/7

Newcastle upon Tyne, its Growth and Achievement, Sydney Middlebrook, Newcastle Journal 1950

Prisons

The State of the Prisons in England and Wales, by John Howard, 1776-1792.

A History of English Prison Administration 1750-1877, by Sean McConville, Routledge, Keegan and Paul, 1981

The Fabrication of Virtue; English Prison Architecture 1750-1840, by Robin Evans, Cambridge UP 1982

Punishments

Bygone Punishments by William Andrews 1899

Of Bridles and Burnings, The Punishment of Women, by E.J. Burford and Sandra Shulman, Hale 1992

Transportation of Convicts

Convicts and the Colonies by A.G.L.Shaw, Faber and Faber 1966

The Fatal Shore by Robert Hughes, Collins Harvill, 1987.

The Complete Book of Emigrants in Bondage 1614-1775 by Peter Wilson Coldham Genealogical Pub. Corp. Baltimore, 1988

Emigrants in Chains by Peter Wilson Coldham, Allan Smith, 1992

The Slave Trade, The History of the Atlantic Slave Trade 1440-1870 by Hugh Thomas, Picador 1997

Crime in the 18th Century

The London Hanged by Peter Linebaugh, Allen Lane, Penguin Press 1991.

The Hanging Tree by V.C.A. Gatrell, Oxford UP 1994

The Thieves Opera by Lucy Moore, Penguin 1998

Rogues, Thieves and the Rule of Law by Gwenda Morgan and Peter Rushton, UCL Press 1998

Life in the 18th Century

England in the Eighteenth Century by P.H. Plumb, Pelican 1950

London Life in the Eighteenth Century by M Dorothy George, Penguin 1966

Eighteenth-Century Newcastle by P.M. Horsley, Oriel Press 1971

Tyneside newspapers, City Library, Newcastle upon Tyne

Index of people mentioned in the text